*The
Agatha
Christie
Companion*

The
Agatha
Christie
Companion

Russell H. Fitzgibbon

Bowling Green State University Popular Press
Bowling Green, Ohio 43403

For
Alan
in whose conversion to a Christiephile I had a part
and who gave constant encouragement and varied
assistance in the preparation of this study

CONTENTS

Preface

My first introduction to the fascinating world of Agatha Christie was, as I recall, through either *The Murder of Roger Ackroyd* or *Ten Little Indians;* in either case, it was one of her classics. And whichever it was—I was hooked. Mrs. Christie, I quickly found, was habit forming. In following years I acquired, I think, all of her detective and mystery stories. Some I liked better than others; none, I can truthfully say, really let me down or left me cold.

Over the years I have read a good many detective stories by a considerable number of authors. Some were exercises in erudition, frameworks for displaying their authors' knowledge of one or another arcane subject. Others were parades of sadism or sex or both. Some were thin skeletons fleshed out with verbiage to book length. Others were unconscionably confused or poorly organized or implausible or trite and tired or trashy. Agatha Christie's stories are very, very rarely subject to such criticisms. The novels and short stories wear well. Proof of this is found in the fact that almost any large bookstore will have, in hardcover or paperback or both, a wide range of Christies even going back to *The Mysterious Affair at Styles* (1920). They obviously wouldn't be stocked if they weren't sold, nor would they be bought if they weren't read. What other authors, in any genre, could present a sustained productive career of more than half a century?

Her death early in 1976 left a void impossible to fill. We were promised one or two posthumous volumes and then new production from that wonderful pen—or typewriter— would be forever ended. But her books will continue to be read—and read—and read.

It is my hope that this guide to her detective and mystery books and short stories will help as a roadmap for Christie *aficionados.* If so, I shall be content.

R.H.F.

The Genre of the Detective Story: Its Nature and Development

What is a "detective story?"

Its name is legion. It is often (as in this volume) made almost synonymous with the mystery story. It is not unrelated to the horror story or the gothic tale. Supernatural, ghost, witch, or vampire stories sometimes move in the same company. Spy and intrigue stories are akin. Science fiction makes contact at some points. Those omnium-gatherums *thriller* and *whodunit* have in recent decades come in to complicate the vocabulary. Must we, then, accept all this melange as "detective" stories? The term will certainly be of little help, indeed, if it must be stretched so broadly.

S.S. Van Dine (Willard Huntington Wright) asserts in his introduction to *The World's Great Detective Stories* (1927) that there are four varieties of popular novels: the romantic, the adventure, the mystery, and the detective; and he adds that "Of these four kinds . . . the detective novel is the youngest, the most complicated, the most difficult of construction, and the most distinct." His point was ably seconded by Edmund Crispin, who wrote in his introduction to *Best Detective Stories* (1959) that "the fully evolved detective story is by far the trickiest form of fiction humanity has so far devised."

As a tentative working definition, let us say with all appropriate diffidence, that a detective story involves the presentation of a *puzzle* (make a mental translation to "crime") and the subsequent solution of the puzzle (substitute here the detection of the criminal and the relevant circumstances associated with the crime). Unless these elements are present, at least in broad essence, we are scarcely justified in applying the label of detective story.

If other constituents are admitted, we progressively dilute the definition until it becomes virtually meaningless. If the "detective" story, whether a novel or a short story or a novella (a "long short"), stresses aspects of horror or an examination of the psychology of the suspects or a large dose

1

of comedy (especially broad comedy) or love interest or social or economic crusading, it falls short in greater or lesser degree of being a detective story in its purest form. That is the formula in brief: the setting up of a crime and then its solution with the "how" and probably the "why" included. It probably should go without saying that the solution is more important than the presentation of the crime. Howard Haycraft put it neatly more than three decades ago in *Murder for Pleasure*: "The crime in a detective story is only the means to an end which is—detection."

Now let us hasten to add a gloss which should be so obvious as to justify the borrowing of a famous phrase, "elementary, my dear Watson": very few detective stories will be found in the pure form suggested by this definition. Most will include in some degree material that we would label mystery (however we may define that term) or the supernatural or horror (or at least terror) or other emotions or forces.

The matter of length is another problem facing the writer who has devised an ingenious plot: what, then, a book or a short story? In his introduction to *The Delights of Detection* (1961), Jacques Barzun makes out a case for the short story, and indeed devotes his entire anthology to short stories. On the other hand, Dorothy L. Sayers in her introduction to *The Second Omnibus of Crime* (1932) takes the opposite point of view, writing that "The detective short story...is in the position of a city built between the sea and a precipice. On the one side it is being gradually undermined, while circumstances prevent its expansion on the other."

How the story grew.

Sayers in her penetrating introduction to *The Omnibus of Crime* (1929) maintained that "Both the detective-story proper and the pure tale of horror are very ancient in origin." The first four stories in her impressive collection are from the Jewish Apocrypha, Herodotus, and *The Aeneid*. But on examination it is seen that these, though they deal with puzzles, do not fall within the purview of the definition advanced above. Doubtless, some elements of puzzle-solution could be found in various stories over the next two millennia. Certainly this is true of some of the writings of Chaucer, Voltaire, and François (Eugene) Vidocq (1775-1857). The third of these, a Parisian criminal turned police spy, was the founder of the French Sûréte and later established the first modern detective agency. Eugene Sue (1804-57) and Dumas *père* (1802-70) approached but did not quite reach the status of detective story writers.

Sayers asserted that the birth of the detective story *per se* had to await the establishment of effective police organizations in England and the United States. Partly true. But that is not the whole story. Though not the obstetrician or the midwife for the modern detective story, certainly its pediatrician was the social and economic changes coming in the middle decades of the nineteenth century. The world was growing smaller. The telegraph, railroads, the development of photography, especially its adoption by newspapers, and perhaps above all, the spread of popular education and its contribution to widening literacy were all factors that helped promote the growth of the detective story as a literary form.

The birth of the modern detective story.

It is an American, that inventive and tortured genius, Edgar Allan Poe (1809-49), who can fairly be called the father of the modern detective story. The word "detective" had not yet come into vocabularies on either side of the Atlantic when Poe wrote the first of his "tales of ratiocination" (his own fond phrase), which established him as the sire of the modern genre. Few American cities had anything resembling organized police machinery. Scotland Yard had not yet established a detective department.

The five stories by which Poe confirmed his paternity over the new literary form were "The Murders in the Rue Morgue" (1841), "The Mystery of Marie Roget" (1842), "The Gold Bug" (1843), "Thou Art the Man" (1844), and "The Purloined Letter" (1845). The tales are not of equal value or importance and do not require individual comment. Some literary historians would reduce the five to a quartet by omitting "Thou Art the Man." Poe's stories established at least three firsts in the detective story formula that would be influential for almost a century thereafter. The first "detective" was created in the person of the Chevalier C. Auguste Dupin, a worthy ancestor of Holmes, Poirot, and many others. Poe also introduced the device of the "idiot friend," the narrator and to some extent the foil of Dupin. In the trilogy of Dupin stories the friend remains unnamed, but he is, of course, the precursor of Watson, Hastings, and others of their ilk. Finally, "The Murders in the Rue Morgue" was the first story of the type known as "locked-room mysteries." Perhaps a fourth innovating contribution of Poe's might be added: "The Purloined Letter" is built around the device of the obvious clue that is overlooked because it *is* so obvious.

All in all, Poe's contribution was a rich one indeed. Critics have picked at flaws in the logic of some of the stories, but there is no gainsaying that the art of the detective story was advanced immeasurably by what Poe wrote.

Post-Poe.

As Symons points out (in *Mortal Consequences*), the flowering of the detective story in the second half of the nineteenth century was in significant degree attributable to the proliferation in England and the United States of a middle class with more leisure and more money. Then, too, the growth of literacy inevitably created wider audiences for detective stories as well as other writing. The spread of education was resisted by some legislators, especially in England, where Pope's dictum that "a little learning is a dangerous thing" still had its adherents (after all, the lower classes must be kept in their place, and literacy certainly would not aid in *that*), but they had as much chance of success as did Canute when he bade the tide go back.

The increase in number and reduction in price of newspapers led to growth in circulation and, incidentally, to stimulation (at least in England) of serialization of novels. Thus were born the "penny dreadfuls"—rather a misnomer. They and their American cousins, the "dime novels," combined to give much popular fiction a black eye which stigmatized many detective stories.

In the meantime, police organization improved on both sides of the Atlantic. Sir Robert Peel, whose names were converted into common-noun synonyms for *police* (i.e., "bobbies" and "peelers") did much to upgrade police work in England. No comparable improvement was to be seen, nationwide, in the United States, but the establishment of the private William J. Burns Detective Agency in the latter nineteenth century did much to improve the image of the efficiency of detectives, even though its operatives were frequently used for strike-breaking. A similar and perhaps even greater reputation, both good and bad, was achieved by the Pinkerton National Detective Agency.

With the public attitude toward the police gradually changing for the better, especially in England, the criminal came to be viewed as an enemy of society rather than a hero or a modern-day Robin Hood. This in time had its inevitable effect on detective-story writing.

In the third quarter of the nineteenth century, a few well known detective-story writers came to public notice. In France, where popular attitudes toward the police differed from those across the Channel—note Hugo's differentiation between the "criminal," Jean Valjean, and the policeman, Javert—the only one of consequence was Emile Gaboriau (1835-73), a popular but not a great writer of novels of detection. A more eminent writer in the genre was a contemporary in England, (William) Wilkie Collins (1824-89). His two outstanding contributions were *The Woman in White* (1860) and, especially, *The Moonstone* (1868). The latter makes good reading, as a detective story, even now, more than a century after its writing, and can perhaps be thought of as the first detective novel written in English. Its detective, Sergeant Cuff, doesn't quite measure up to Collins's buildup of him, but nonetheless he was a sleuth of no mean ability.

The same field of writing in the United States was relatively barren at that period, but was notable for the appearance of the first prominent woman writer of detective stories, Anna Katharine Green (1846-1935). Her writing was highly popular during the Victorian era but was marked by sentimentality and moralizing.

Sherlock Holmes arrives.

Then, in the later 1880s and the early 1890s, a new star appeared in the firmament and soon began shining like a nova. Arthur Conan Doyle (1895-1930) took a degree in medicine in 1885. He opened an office for his practice in Southsea, but the world, or even Southsea or later London, did not beat a path to his door. Christopher Morley in his introduction to *The Complete Sherlock Holmes* (1938) pays tribute to those who walked by his doorway: "A blessing, then, on those ophthalmic citizens who did not go to that office. . .where in 1891 Dr. A. Conan Doyle set up consulting rooms as an eye specialist. It was there, waiting for the patients who never came, that he began to see the possibilities in Sherlock Holmes. No wonder that Dr. Watson too sometimes rather neglected his practice."

In the absence of those patients who would provide the guineas he might throw at the wolf, Doyle, at Southsea before removing to London, began making notes for story characters who might eke out his existence. He planned for an Ormond Sacker from Afghanistan, a doctor, who would share digs with Sherrinford Holmes. *A Study in Scarlet* was duly written and published in *Beeton's Christmas Annual* for 1887; it was not notably successful, even though it included Holmes. By that time, fortunately, Sacker and Sherrinford Holmes had been metamorphosed into Dr. John H. Watson and Sherlock Holmes. Other books followed in 1888, 1889, and 1891; not one was a literary earthquake.

Then in July, 1891, Doyle published in *The Strand Magazine* the first of a series of six Holmes short stories. Immediately the stars of both author and detective were in the ascendant. Short stories were at the time much more in vogue than novels as a fiction format and most of the Holmes appearances were in short-story form—fifty-six of them over the years as against four novels. In contrast, we follow Poirot in thirty-three novels and fifty-four short stories.

Despite his occasional resort to cocaine or opium, Holmes is a man normally above human emotions or frailties. He is egotistical—he had a low opinion of the abilities of Poe's Dupin and Gaboriau's Lecoq—but he did not have the comical vanity of Poirot. As a detective he is definitely three-dimensional, and he seldom lets us down, though a number of the stories of the 1920s are less gripping than earlier ones.

Post-Holmes.

It was inevitable that the comet-like popularity of Doyle and his creation would stimulate further good writing in the detective-story form. Only a few of the most eminent successors need be mentioned in this capsule survey. The English writer Gilbert K. Chesterton (1874-1936) won literary credentials in a number of fields—poetry, polemical journalism, drama writing, literary criticism—as well as in the production of much-above-average detective short stories. His great contribution in the latter field was the diminutive, unassuming Catholic priest, Father Brown. The little father was unorthodox in his violation of the canons of detective-construction of that day, but he quickly caught the fancy of the public.

Jacques Futrelle (1875-1912)—born in Georgia rather than France, but actually a Canadian—became momentarily popular through his invention of Professor Augustus S.F.X. Van Dusen, the "thinking machine." The Van Dusen stories were ingenious, but lacked logic and plausibility. Ernest Bramah (Smith) (1878-1942) was noteworthy chiefly because of his creation of the blind detective Max Carrados. But Carrados was not the best of the breed in the post-Holmes period. R(ichard) Austin Freeman (1862-1943), an English writer with medical training, gave detective-story fans perhaps the first really scientific detective or forensic scientist in the person of Dr. John E. Thorndyke. The investigative accomplishments of Dr. Thorndyke were plausible and convincing, but Freeman's writing itself was not exceptional.

During and after World War I, the short story was giving way to the detective novel in popularity. The appeal of the latter to women became more pronounced, and one of the first writers to capitalize on the trend was the prolific and immensely successful Mary Roberts Rinehart (1876-1958). Her murder novels, her favorite kind, did not exploit a single detective alone, with the partial exception of Nurse Pinkerton (possibly some significance in the choice of that name), but they had widespread appeal. From the appearance of *The Circular Staircase* (1908, her second book) she was for years one of the most popular writers in the United States.

The Golden Age.

Just as it is difficult to say precisely when the Middle Ages began, it is a problem to determine with anything like unanimity of acceptance the beginning date of the "golden age" of detective-story writing. Did that period begin in 1920 with the publication of Agatha Christie's *The Mysterious Affair at Styles* or in 1926 with her *The Murder of Roger Ackroyd* or perhaps in 1925, a conveniently "round" date in mid-decade? Take your choice. At any rate, Agatha Christie would seem to be undeniably related to the onset of the age. *Styles* was not a publishing sensation, at least at the time, but *Ackroyd* definitely was; it even gave rise later to the adjective *ackroidal,* which has gained some acceptance among devotees of the genre.

The decade of the '20s drew more critical attention to the detective story as a literary form than had previously been given it. Quality definitely began to improve; the detective story was graduating from the level of *Captain Billy's Whiz Bang* and *The Police Gazette.* By the end of the decade, a fairly generally accepted set of boundary lines for the form had evolved. The detective story was definitely to be a game; it must provide clues; the detective, by rational analysis of the clues and without employment of intuition, coincidence, or use of information not made available to the reader, must arrive at a plausible solution of the puzzle, i.e., he must solve the crime. The author should refrain from becoming emotionally involved with his hero-detective. The development of such a format put the detective himself front and center in the structure of the story and, especially as the short story gave way to the novel, it meant that murder was the most feasible crime to be used. Other unofficial "rules" developed, some of them fairly detailed, but they need not detain us.

Other characteristics of the golden age were important, though they were not rules for writing in the sense of those mentioned in the preceding paragraph. Granted that detective stories were essentially "escape literature," what was written in the 1920s and '30s very largely ignored social, economic, and political currents, whether they were small eddies or more ominous riptides. Thus much of the detective story writing of the time seemed to be in a sort of never-never land that was oblivious of unemployment and labor unrest, economic boom and then depression, the growing emancipation of women, nascent fascism, and other disturbances of various kinds. Julian Symons put it well in *Mortal Consequences:* "The fairy-tale land of the Golden Age was one in which murder was committed over and over without anybody getting hurt."

One of the successful leaders in the field was Anthony Berkeley (Cox) (1893-1970), who later used the pseudonym Francis Iles. Although Berkeley-Iles did not always adhere to the conventions of detective-story construction, his writing was lively and is still highly readable.

Certainly one of the outstanding writers of the golden

age was Dorothy L. Sayers (1893-1957), whose career as a detective-story writer was short (1923-36) though brilliant; after 1936 she devoted her writing to Anglican church matters. Her chief addition to the directory of detectives was Lord Peter Wimsey, who was fatuous and foppish. He was not as much so as Wodehouse's Bertie Wooster, but then Wodehouse intended Wooster to be ridiculous and there is convincing evidence that Miss Sayers admired the personality she gave Wimsey. Julian Symons suggests that she "might have been a better and livelier crime writer if she had not fallen in love with her detective." Nonetheless, her writing was ingenious and workmanlike, though verbose and snobbish. Not the least of the Sayers contributions was her editing of two notable anthologies, *The Omnibus of Crime* (1928) and *The Second Omnibus of Crime* (1932). A less notable *Third Omnibus* followed.

The principal American luminary during the golden age was Willard Huntington Wright (1888-1939), who wrote his detective novels under the name of S.S. Van Dine. He had good credentials as an art and music critic and his erudition in these and related areas was genuine. His meteoric rise as a detective-story writer was built around the character of Philo Vance, an affected and snobbish dilettante who was a fitting counterpart to the British Wimsey. Vance introduced too much of his learning into his series of novels, beginning with *The Benson Murder Case* (1926) and continuing through a succession of other *Murder Cases,* respectively: *Canary, Greene, Bishop, Scarab, Dragon, Casino, Kidnap, Gracie Allen, Garden,* and *Winter.* (Someone pointed out that, perhaps coincidentally and with one exception, the differentiating words in his titles each contained six letters.) The meteor that flashed so rapidly paled almost as quickly; the later novels were much inferior to the early ones. Ogden Nash concluded that

> Philo Vance
> Needs a kick in the pance.

The golden age continued through the 1930s with other additions to the list of top-flight writers. One (or should one say two?) of the newcomers was Ellery Queen. Queen was in reality the principal pseudonym of two Brooklyn-born cousins, Frederic Dannay (1905-) and Manfred B. Lee (1905-

71). This was a long and successful collaboration which in original writing, editing, and the publication of a long-lived mystery magazine has been truly unique. The pseudonymous author Queen is also the detective-hero of the many stories the cousins wrote. Many of the novels were exercises in perfection of construction. *The Ellery Queen Mystery Magazine* began publication in 1941 and is now more than a third of a century old; in 1960 it began issuing annual anthologies.

A writer whom many thought of, probably unjustly, as little more than a hack because of his enormous productivity and the uniformity of his formats was Erle Stanley Gardner (1889-1970), whose famous detective was Perry Mason, given greater immortality on the television screen by Raymond Burr. Gardner, who used pseudonyms (and under them somewhat variant formats), specialized in cases involving courtroom scenes, in which his score of years as a practicing lawyer stood him in good stead. His stories were almost always marked by fast-paced dialogue.

Another outstanding figure was John Dickson Carr (1905-77), who also wrote under the name of Carter Dickson. An American, he lived in England for almost two decades. Carr and his detective, Dr. Gideon Fell, exploit especially the device of the locked-room murder. A prolific producer of detective novels, whose writing goes back to the 1920s, was Rex Stout (1886-1975). His classic detective, Nero Wolfe, rivals Carr's Dr. Fell, in obesity at least. Some critics felt that the quality of Stout's novels began to decline as the years passed, but he remained one of the outstanding detective-story writers until his death.

After the Golden Age.
World War II contributed its meed of disillusionment and cynicism, not only to public and private relationships but also to the changing character of detective-story writing, with Hammett and Chandler as forerunners. Devising of plots and then their execution lapsed badly from what had prevailed earlier. Corrupt or sadistic policemen (or both) became commonplace in the newer writing. Sex was treated with unwonted frankness and was often accompanied by perversion and lechery. Four-letter words illustrated a sort of literary Gresham's law: "bad" words tend to drive out "good" words.

An oversimplified summary of the postwar period was that the detective story gave way to the crime novel. Symons in *Mortal Consequences* (p. 178-80) footnotes the change. The solving of a puzzle (crime), characteristic of the golden age, suffered in the transition.

Although his writing of detective novels was done in the late 1920s, (Samuel) Dashiell Hammett (1894-1961) really belongs to the later period. Though his detectives Sam Spade and Nick Charles were not the pathological killers that some later writers introduced, they were hard-boiled and hard-bitten and can be thought of as precursors of many of the post-World War II detectives. The best of Hammett's limited output were *The Red Harvest, The Maltese Falcon, The Glass Key,* and *The Thin Man.* Similar to Hammett but less tough and probably less effective was Raymond Chandler (1888-1959). His writing was sharp and his detective, Philip Marlowe, convincing. Mickey Spillane (Frank Morrison 1918-) and his Mike Hammer represent perhaps an apogee of sadism and violence. There is little detection in his writing.

Miscellany.

As to *women in the business,* they can be there either as sleuths or authors. In the former capacity, they began with Anna Katharine Green's Violet Strange. Dorothy Sayers herself admitted (in *The Omnibus of Crime*) that "on the whole, they have not been very successful" (and here we must give our apologies to Miss Marple). The women detectives are, Miss Sayers said, "irritatingly intuitive," "active and courageous,...hampering the men engaged on the job," or subject to the risk that "marriage looms too large in their view of life; which is not surprising, for they are all young and beautiful."

As writers, however, women have earned a distinguished place in the development of the genre. Some have been mentioned previously, others not. A baker's dozen of eminent writers, obviously by no means all of those deserving mention, will footnote the statement:

Anna Katharine Green (1846-1935); Baroness Emmuska Orczy (1865-1947); Marie-Adelaide Belloc Lowndes (1868-1947); Carolyn Wells (1869-1942); Mary Roberts Rinehart (1876-1958); Agatha Christie (1890-1976); Dorothy Sayers (1393-1957); Josephine Tey (1896-1952); Ngaio Marsh (1899-

); Mignon Eberhart (1899-); Georgette Heyer (1902-74); Margery Allingham (1904-66); Margaret Millar (1915-). They, and other women writers, have truly made outstanding contributions to detective fiction.

Detective-story writing has not at all been an Anglo-American monopoly, although writers in these two countries have dominated it. It could flourish only in countries having a free or reasonably free intellectual atmosphere and those immune from governmental restraints and censorship over writing. It goes almost without saying that we cannot look to Communist-controlled countries for detective story writing. If approached theoretically, the explanation might be that since Communist societies are supposedly near perfect and hence without crime or criminals, it is futile to waste their energies by writing detective stories. Doubtless more important is the pragmatic reason that writing cleverly devised stories of the kind could put ideas into the heads of potentially inclined criminal types who, despite the happy theory, just might be found here and there.

Another element in the picture is the fact that in recent generations the English language had become so widely understood among educated people in other European countries that they either read detective stories in English by preference or they were able to translate them into their own languages.

For many years France was virtually the only non-English-speaking country to make contributions to this literary form. A few Frenchmen have been mentioned in preceding pages—Voltaire, Vidocq, Sue, Dumas, Gaboriau—but most of them were pioneers who made only fragmentary contributions or else were second-rate writers. One who deserves a few more lines is that contemporary phenomenon, the Belgian author writing in French, Georges (Joseph Christian) Simenon (1903-), and his creation, Inspector Jules Maigret.

Not all of Simenon's large output of novels involves Maigret, but the Inspector is his detectival trademark. Simenon's writing is sharp and his character portrayal realistic and convincing. It is Maigret who speaks for Simenon; he is, in a sense, an alter ego of his creator and seems to have a personality apart from that of the author. Simenon makes his creation bourgeois and essentially conservative; he gives him energy and endless patience.

Aside from the French, pre-eminently Simenon (if we may assign him to France), Continental Europe has produced few other detective writers of note. There is some evidence that Switzerland, the Scandinavian countries, the Netherlands, and Italy may have budding writers of promise, but so far they can be counted on one's fingers, with several digits to spare.

If one thinks that the eighty-four detective and mystery books written by Agatha Christie constitute a record for productivity, he must revise his conclusions. That is no mean accomplishment, it is true, especially when quality is coupled with numbers, but it is not a sheer numerical record. We cannot present an exhaustive catalog of *the Big Producers,* but we will present a few illustrations. Erle Stanley Gardner (1889-1970) is estimated to have written 120 books; the estimate may be conservative. E(dward) Phillips Oppenheim (1866-1946) produced 115 novels and thirty-nine books of short stories. Carolyn Wells (1869-1942) wrote 175 books, of which seventy-five dealt with crime and mystery. (Richard H.) Edgar Wallace (1875-1932) was just under that record, having written 173 books, about half of them dealing with mystery and crime. J(oseph) S(mith) Fletcher (1863-1935) wrote more than a hundred detective novels. But all records pale beside that of John Creasey (1908-73). Up to 1968, so Barzun and Taylor tell us (in *A Catalogue of Crime*), he had published 521 books under twenty-one names!

Selected Bibliography on the Genre

Ball, John (ed.). *The Mystery Story.* San Diego: University of California, San Diego, 1976. An invaluable collection of essays—historical, analytical, bibliographic—on the genre; published by University Extension.

Barzun, Jacques. "Detection and the Literary Art." Introduction to *The Delights of Detection.* New York: Criterion Books, 1961, pp. 9-23. A study of the relation of the detective short story (of which the volume is an anthology) to literature.

Barzun, Jacques and **Wendell H. Taylor.** *A Catalogue of Crime* (second impression corrected). New York: Harper and Row, 1971. A "critical survey of some 7,500 works," this indispensable volume is as nearly complete as anything in print.

Hagen, Ordean A. *Who Done It? A Guide to Detective, Mystery, and Suspense Fiction.* New York and London: Bowker, 1969. Comprehensive but erratic and with numerous errors and omissions.

Haycraft, Howard (ed.). *The Art of the Mystery Story.* New York: Simon and Schuster, 1946. An excellent collection of more than fifty essays on detective and mystery fiction.

Haycraft, Howard. *Murder for Pleasure: The Life and Times of the Detective Story.* New York: D. Appleton-Century, 1941. A first-rate, thorough analysis of the genre.

Sayers, Dorothy L. (ed.). *The Omnibus of Crime.* New York: Payson and Clark, 1929. The Introduction, pp. 9-46, gives an excellent survey, chiefly chronological, of the development of the detective or crime story.

Sayers, Dorothy L. (ed.). *The Second Omnibus of Crime: The World's Great Crime Stories.* New York: Blue Ribbon Books, 1932. The Introduction to this second of Miss Sayers's anthologies, pp. 1-16, is a penetrating discussion of detective-story growth, construction, psychology, and other aspects.

Scott, Sutherland. *Blood in Their Ink.* London: Stanley Paul, 1953. A comprehensive description of modern mystery and detective novels.

Symons, Julian. *Mortal Consequences: A History—From the Detective Story to the Crime Novel.* New York: Harper and Row, 1972. A good survey; critical of many popular writers.

Steinbrunner, Chris and **Otto Penzler** (eds.). *Encyclopedia of Mystery and Detection.* New York: McGraw-Hill, 1976. An encompassing collection of information about the genre.

Thomson, H(enry) Douglas. *Masters of Mystery.* London: Collins, 1931. A fundamental analysis even though more than four decades old.

Van Dine, S.S. (Willard Huntington Wright). "The Detective Story." Introduction to *The World's Great Detective Stories.* New York: Blue Ribbon Books, 1927, pp. 3-27. Van Dine writes as a critic and shows a good knowledge of the development of the genre.

Wells, Carolyn. *The Technique of the Mystery Story.* Springfield, Mass.: Home Correspondence School, 1913. A very solid, pioneer work.

Dame Agatha Christie

Dame Agatha Christie in 1971 was officially recognized as a daughter of Britain. In that year she was made a D.B.E.—a Dame Commander, Order of the British Empire. But long before that some unofficial and invisible literary College of Arms had elevated her to the peerage. Probably her escutcheon showed crossed daggers and coshes, a dripping vial of poison, and similar appropriate devices. The insignia displayed dexter would not be of so much note, but those shown sinister were—well sinister. Dame Agatha has been variously dubbed the Duchess of Death, the Mistress of Mystery, the Queen of Crime. We don't suggest the addition of the Baroness of Blood or the Marchioness of Mayhem, but doubtless those or other alliterative epithets will be proposed to show the near royal esteem in which millions of her readers hold her.

This recognition—and many other evidences of it can be cited—indicates that Mrs. Christie, as most people still call her, is to be thought of both as an institution and a phenomenon. Detective and mystery story writers are more than legion, but there has been only one Agatha Christie. Total sales of her books, we are told, exceed 400 million copies and, one of her New York publishers informs us (basing his statement on a 1962 U.N. report), her books have been translated into 103 foreign languages, sixteen more than Shakespeare can claim.

The encomiums and superlatives might be multiplied—Pelion atop Ossa—at great length, but it is sufficient for the moment to say that she is authoritatively regarded as the most widely read author in the English language today.

*   *   *

Agatha Mary Clarissa Miller was born at Torquay, Devonshire, on September 15, 1890. For years there was confusion about her birth year, which she herself did nothing to correct. For years, too, neither the British nor the

American *Who's Who* listed a year for her birth, and many biographies and library catalogs gave it as 1891. The scores upon scores of author cards in the Library of Congress catalog listed 1891 as her birth year, at least until the Library's attention was called to the error in 1975; perhaps a correction has not yet been made.

The family was a comfortable, middle-sized, middle-class one, product of an Anglo-American marriage. Her father, Frederick Alvah Miller (from New York), she once described as "a very amusing father, always doing nothing." He died when she was eleven years of age. Her charming but eccentric English mother was left in charge of her rearing. The mother was, Dame Agatha later wrote, "an intelligent woman with a very original mind. She had the gift of awakening enthusiasm on a subject, and my education in her hands (I had no governess and did not go to school) became a thrilling game." Even as a child Agatha liked time to herself, read widely in romances—and Sherlock Holmes!—and invented imaginary playmates who to her were much more alive than the neighboring children who at times came to play.

Her fertile imagination led also to the devising of many mental stories, but they were not transferred to paper until one occasion when she had a cold and could not go outdoors. For diversion, her mother told her, "You'd better write a story." It was not easy then, she admits, but it became more so as time passed. All these early literary efforts, she says, were very sad and sentimental; she saw to it that most of her characters died off before the stories ended.

Dame Agatha's education depended on the current enthusiasms of her mother. In those years, the waning ones of Victoria's reign, it was usual for girls to be taught at home and "classes" normally did not go beyond piano, dancing, and cooking. Her mother shocked neighbors by sending Agatha's older sister to a rather progressive girls' school at Brighton, but by the time Agatha herself might have gone her mother had decided that formal education was hard on a child's eyes and brains and so she was kept at home.

She did get some formal training beginning at age sixteen, when her mother sent her to Paris for two years to study singing and piano. The experience was useful. Her facility with the piano greatly increased, although not to concert dimensions. Her voice, she found, was not strong enough for operatic roles, nor would her shyness allow her to stand up in public. That shyness also tended to tie her tongue. On one occasion a young man returned her to her mother after a dance and commented to her mother, "Well, you daughter can dance, but she hasn't learned to talk yet." An incidental dividend of the Parisian years was her improved facility with French, a knowledge that permitted her to endow Poirot with his delightfully fractured English, interlaced with French, in his early book and short-story appearances.

In 1912 Agatha became engaged to Archibald Christie, a handsome young officer in what in 1918 became the R.A.F. Two years later, on December 24, 1914, they were married. Her husband was stationed in France and as her own contribution to the war effort, Mrs. Christie entered the Voluntary Aid Detachment and took up service in a hospital at Torquay. A further dividend occurred there. As a part of her hospital service toward the end of the war, she worked in the dispensary, where she became familiar with many of the poisons she employed so effectively in the wholesale literary murders she would later commit.

In the meantime she had wetted her feet in fiction writing. Her mother had taken her to Cairo for a winter and there—laboriously, she confesses—she had written a novel. Her hospital work during the war gave her little time for writing until near the end of the conflict, but she did manage to write a few short stories, some of which, to her excitement and pleasure, were published. (She later dedicated her *Pocket Full of Rye* to Bruce Ingram, "who liked and published my first short stories.") A Torquay neighbor and family friend, Eden Phillpotts, the distinguished Devonshire writer (twenty-eight years the senior of Christie), gave her consistent encouragement in her efforts.

A discussion with her older sister in 1916 about the genre of detective stories led to the sister's lament that it was nigh impossible to find a good detective story, one in which the reader could not easily guess the criminal. Mrs. Christie thought she could write one, her sister doubted it, and, faced by such a challenge, she began work on *The Mysterious Affair at Styles*. The date should have signified a milestone in the annals of literary criminality, but for years the opus was destined to blush unseen, or rather unread—it languished in manuscript. For one thing, the writing was slow going; it had to be done in fits and snatches squeezed from her hospital work. But, when she accrued a two-week leave from hospital duties, she went out to stay by herself on Dartmoor and got it finished.

Then began its peddling. Mrs. Christie sent it to a publisher, and in due course it was returned. This happened several times. Not all the publishers in England sent rejection slips, but a discouraging number did. Then she sent it to John Lane at the Bodley Head, which company sat on it for months. She had almost forgotten about it when, nearly a year later, a request came from Lane for an interview; that resulted in a contract and in publication in 1920. Thus was born the inimitable Hercule Poirot, second only to Sherlock Holmes among fictional sleuths, and thus was launched Dame Agatha's remarkable career.

Though Sutherland Scott in *Blood in Their Ink* affirmed that *Styles* "set an immediate standard, as high as any which prevails today (1953)" and that it "must surely be classed. . .as one of the finest 'firsts' ever written," it was not an earth-shaking financial success. It sold about 2,000 copies and, it is reported, netted about twenty-five pounds for its author. It was not published in New York until 1927. But *Styles* did serve the highly consequential end of stimulating its author to continue her writing at an accelerated pace, even though she had published half a dozen books before she finally decided that authorship was an adequate means of livelihood. The first half of the 1920s saw the literary birth of the Beresfords (though not yet married), Superintendent Battle, and Colonel Race; Jane Marple would not appear in book form until 1930. Short stories soon came along.

In 1926 William Collins and Sons, by then Mrs. Christie's primary British publisher, brought out *The Murder of Roger Ackroyd*. It created an immediate sensation. Its critics, both those pro and those con, at once jumped into the battle over the the author's fairness. The reason for the frenetic discussion is of course obvious. As virtually all humankind knows, Mrs. Christie, possibly for the first time, and certainly most dramatically, had pushed the principle that the murderer must be the least likely suspect to its ultimate conclusion: the ostensible narrator of *Ackroyd* is ultimately revealed as himself the murderer.

"This device" (or trick, as the reader may prefer), writes Howard Haycraft, the eminent historiographer of the genre,

in *Murder for Pleasure,* "provoked the most violent debate in
detective story history. Scarcely had the ink dried on the
pages before representatives of one school of thought were
crying, 'Foul play!' Other readers and critics rallied as
ardently to Mrs. Christie's defense, chanting the dictum: 'It
is the reader's business to suspect *every one.*' The question
remains unsettled today [1941], and the inconclusive
argument will probably continue as long as detective stories
are read and discussed." The pro-Christie forces gradually
won the day, and it is now generally conceded that the
gambit, though novel, was entirely legitimate. Writes Scott
in *Blood in Their Ink*: "The ingenuity which suggested this
format, which maintained the cloak of secrecy to the very
last moment, deserves the highest commendation. If Agatha
Christie had made no other contribution to the literature of
detective fiction she would still deserve our grateful thanks."

But Mrs. Christie was being overtaken by events. Soon
after the publication of *Ackroyd* her mother suddenly died.
She was also faced with the impending disintegration of her
own marriage to Colonel Christie, C.M.G., D.S.O. The
pressures were more than she could bear. On the morning of
December 4, 1926, she left her Berkshire house, Styles
(named for her first Poirot book), to go for a drive. Alarmed
by her failure to return after an appropriate time, her
husband called the police and a search was at once begun.
Concern was heightened two days later when her car was
found with its front wheels hanging over a cliff.

Public interest in the case was increased, of course, by
the fact that it was a leading mystery writer who had
disppeared. The case might, indeed, have come out of one of
her own books. Sensational columnists were quick to
advance the hypothesis that the disappearance was staged
to promote sales of those books. Rumors flew in all
directions; one of the more dramatic was a report to police
that a man on the day after the disappearance had met a
woman near the scene, obviously recently crying, with hair
disheveled; he was certain it was Mrs. Christie. Virtually the
whole country took up the search for the missing writer,
guided by detectives, amateur and professional, and aided
by bloodhounds and beagles, airplanes and tractors, and
15,000 volunteers.

The climax came a fortnight after her disappearance
when staff members in a Yorkshire spa hotel in the north of

England noticed the considerable resemblance between published pictures of the missing writer and one of the hotel guests, registered as Teresa Neele of Capetown. (Oddly, the name was that of the woman who became the second wife of Colonel Christie.) "Mrs. Neele" seemed entirely normal and had often participated in after-dinner musicals organized by hotel guests. Police were called and the woman in question was quickly identified as Mrs. Christie herself. Doctors who examined her determined it to be a genuine loss of memory— "a classic case of amnesia resulting from overstrain."

Although the lost two weeks were thus proved to be no fake, the publicity results of the case were predictably just the same as if they had been: bookstore stocks of her earlier works were quickly sold out, two newspapers began serializing her stories, and her name was on everyone's tongue. Poirot, at the moment, anyway, was certainly of more note than Sherlock Holmes, even though the doyen of Baker Street and his creator were both still living.

Mrs. Christie was divorced from her husband in 1928 (Colonel Christie died in 1962) and spent much of the next two years traveling while her daughter Rosalind was in school. In 1930 she visited Ur (of the Chaldees) in what is now Iraq and there met Max Edgar Lucien Mallowan, an archeologist from the University of London, who was assisting Sir Leonard Woolley with his excavations in Mesopotamia. The two were married on September 11, 1930. Thereafter she spent several months of most years in Iraq or Syria aiding her husband with his work there and assuming responsibility for the photography and much of the record keeping.

While in the desert she had only limited time for chronicling the exploits of her various detectives, but the locales did give her the inspiration for several later Poirot novels. They also provided the archeological ore which she mined and displayed for her growing following in the highly readable non-fiction book, *Come, Tell Me How You Live* (1946), a lively account of the pleasures of the "digs."

There had been considerable speculation just after Mrs. Christie's case of amnesia in 1926 that the experience would "finish" her as a writer of top-level detective stories. But within a few months she was again hard at work and high-quality books and short stories continued to flow from her typewriter. In 1930 she brought out the first Westmacott novel, *Giant's Bread*. For years only her family and her publisher were privy to the fact that it was in reality pseudonymous. The year 1934 saw an incredible seven imprints coming out of her fertile typewriter: two Poirot novels, a collection of Pyne short stories, another short-story collection with no central detectives, a novel also without a central sleuth, a Westmacott, and an original play. *Annus mirabilis*.

What Julian Symons, in *Mortal Consequences,* calls the "golden age" of detective-story writing extended from about the middle 1920s to World War II. Four names, he thinks, stand out in the first years of the period: Agatha Christie, Dorothy Sayers, and Anthony Berkeley (Cox) in Britain and S.S. Van Dine (Willard Huntington Wright) in the United States. One might quarrel with his ranking of leaders, but certainly those named were among the first-magnitude stars in the firmament. The prolificness of Christie was suggested in the preceding paragraph; the quality of her writing was equally high. The golden age may fairly be said to have been ushered in with *Ackroyd,* and that book remains one of the great detective stories of all time.

The decade and a half preceding the second World War saw the lives of Mrs. Christie (she retained that name for professional purposes) and her husband falling into a reasonably routine pattern. Summers were usually spent at the Middle Eastern digs—Professor Mallowan became head of the British School of Archeology in Iraq, and was later knighted for his outstanding work there. Mrs. Christie used her winters to concentrate on her writing. Both tried to protect their privacy. Dr. Mallowan has been described as "a short, stout, cheerful professor" at the University of London. He was one of the most distinguished archeologists of our time. His wife's work with him made her more than amateurishly familiar with the technical language of his and related sciences. At the end of *The Man in the Brown Suit,* for example, she has her heroine, the daughter of an anthropologist, engage in a cabled exchange with a friend just after the arrival of the daughter's first-born:

> "Suzanne sent me a cable when he was born:
> *"Congratulations and love to the latest arrival on Lunatics' Island. Is his head dolichocephalic or brachycephalic?"*

"I wasn't going to stand that from Suzanne. I sent her a
reply of one word, economical and to the point:
"*Platycephalic.*"

The very different careers of the two Mallowans were
melded quite harmoniously and to their mutual advantage.
It was undoubtedly inevitable that someone would come up
with the probably contrived story about an archeologist's
wife. But two of the Christie interviewers present her
reactions to it differently. Wrote Nigel Dennis in a *Life*
article in 1956: "...she is fond of quoting the witty wife who
once said, 'an archeologist is the best husband any woman
can have: the older she gets, the more interested he is in
her.'" But Gordon Ramsey in *Agatha Christie: Mistress of
Mystery* puts it differently: "...the remark attributed to
Mrs. Christie that 'the older you get, the more interesting you
become to an archeologist,' was the creation of some pundit
whose neck Mrs. Christie would be glad to wring if he would
care to identify himself—she neither made the remark nor
does she consider it particularly complimentary or
amusing."

World War II brought to the Mallowans, as to all
Britons, great changes. Professor Mallowan joined the
R.A.F. but the Government decided his talents and
experience could be used better as adviser on Arab affairs in
Tripolitania attached to the British military government in
North Africa. As in the first war, Mrs. Christie again served
as a volunteer nurse and was assigned to work in the
dispensary of the University College in London. Again her
knowledge of poisons was broadened. Woe to those criminals
who believed that their familiarity with exotic poisons
would let them escape from her postwar detectives' exploits.

Her war work gave Mrs. Christie little to do in the
evenings and she continued to turn to her typewriter. Two
books were written for presumably posthumous publication.
They were the "last cases" of Hercule Poirot and Jane
Marple, respectively. On the assumption that there was "no
reason the Chancellor of the Exchequer should have all the
benefit," she transferred copyrights to her husband and
daughter with the expectation that by publication of the
books after her death they could take a trip around the world
on the royalties.

But the phenomenal success of the motion picture

Murder on the Orient Express beginning in 1974 (it had already made more money than any other film in British cinema history), changed her mind. The final exploit of Poirot, related in *Curtain,* was published in the fall of 1975 (it had already appeared, condensed, as a two-part serial in a magazine of national circulation in the United States). A nostalgic reception for this valedictory of an enfeebled but still brilliant Poirot was assured and, indeed, the book quickly climbed to the top of the fiction best-seller lists. The Midas-touch still characterized what pertained to Poirot: American paperback book rights to *Curtain* were bought for $925,000.

The final disposition of "the last Marple" was delayed for a year beyond the publication of *Curtain.* In the summer of 1976 the *Ladies' Home Journal* began its publication under the title *Sleeping Murder.* Condensed in the periodical, it was published in complete book form later in the year in both England and the United States. The author also thought of her autobiography, begun in 1950, as a posthumous publication. "If anybody writes about my life in the future," she told interviewer Francis Wyndham, "I'd rather they got the facts right." The autobiography was published late in 1977.

The postwar years inevitably found Poirot and Miss Marple growing older. They were not like Peter Pan and Little Orphan Annie who never aged. As the two of them grew in years, they tended to become more weary and more than once Poirot threatened to retire completely and grow vegetable marrows. As ennui enveloped these and other Christie detectives, some reviewers saw it casting its shadow over the author herself. Indeed, in an interview with Julian Symons in the *London Sunday Times* some years ago, she "sounded wistful and almost depressed" about her work: "'I don't enjoy writing detective stories. I enjoy thinking of a detective story, planning it, but when the time comes to write it, it is like going to work every day, like having a job.'"

Through the years honors came to Agatha Christie. In 1950 she was made a Fellow of the Royal Society of Literature; five years later she received the New York Drama Critics Circle Award. The following year she was made a Commander of the Order of the British Empire. In 1961 the University of Exeter bestowed on her the honorary degree of Doctor of Literature. And in 1972 she was measured for a wax portrait for Madame Tussaud's Museum (the ultimate accolade). Thus Dame Agatha aged gracefully. Her rule was still modest and was, of course, still accepted with entire loyalty by her millions of devoted subjects.

The end of the illustrious career occurred on January 12, 1976, when Dame Agatha died at her home fifty miles west of London. She had been in failing health for the preceding month or two.

Publication some weeks later of the terms of Dame Agatha's will caused surprise on both sides of the Atlantic. It revealed her personal estate to be only £ 106,683, or less than $200,000 at current exchange rates. For an author whose *Curtain* was reputed already to have earned more than a million dollars in royalties and reprint rights and whose recent film *Murder on the Orient Express* was said to have brought in some $80,000,000 in box office returns, an estate of a hundred thousand pounds did indeed seem trifling. The *Saturday Review* (June 26, 1976) speculated that the author's great writing income "apparently...lies buried within a complex honeycomb of holding companies and family trusts, set up over the last twenty years to shield the Christie profits from Britain's tax collectors."

But, regardless of the intricacies of untangling a possibly involved estate, one thing was clear: One of the most distinguished of literary giants had joined the immortals.

*   *   *

How she worked.

A brief "macroview" of how Dame Agatha divided her working time between summers and winters has already been presented. It is now in order to look at her work habits with something of a microscope. Getting ideas for stories was the first problem. No short or simple answer can be given as to where she found those ideas. Willa Petschek wrote in *McCall's Magazine* a few years ago that "One plot occurred to her when she was on an escalator; another while she was gazing at a set of Dresden figurines on her mother's mantelpiece (*Ten Little Niggers?*); still a third when she overheard, in a restaurant, a conversation on statistics. 'I was just beginning a new thriller (the Parker Pyne stories?), and the thought of all those numbers intrigued me.' The fact is that Agatha Christie's ideas come to her wherever she is: darning socks, standing at the stove...or, in the old days, munching apples in her bath—an ancient Victorian affair with a wide mahogany ledge, on which she put her notebooks, cups of tea, pencils, and apple cores (it's easy to see whence Ariadne Oliver inherited her munching habits)... 'But nowadays they don't build baths like that, so I've rather given up the practice.' After attending a performance by Ruth Draper, and subsequently reflecting on how clever her impersonations were, her train of thought finally led Christie to come out with the novel *Lord Edgware Dies.*

The plots did not spring, Athena-like, full-fledged into being from the head of Agatha Christie. Sometimes an idea had to germinate for months or even years (e.g., *Crooked House*) before she was ready to transfer it to paper. The actual writing proceeded rapidly. Working from notes, sitting straight (a la Miss Marple) in a Chippendale chair before a portable typewriter, she usually managed to turn out a novel in a month-and-a-half to three months. In a number of years in the 1930s her production of whodunits was two annually. Writing quickly, she found, produced more spontaneity and minimized the interruptions that seemed to crowd in on her. The quick writing was important from a practical, scheduling angle: to get a book ready for publication in November—the "Christie for Christmas"—she had to turn over the manuscript by March. Springs, then, could be used for stoking up energy, the summers for the "digs" in the Middle East. She called herself "a perfect sausage machine."

Her plots had to be developed in reverse, that is, she had first to determine the climax or denouement and then work backward from there. The construction of plays, whether originals or adaptations from her novels, required necessary changes in technique from that used in writing the novels themselves. She learned a number of important lessons early about writing her novels: the murder, if there was to be one, should be introduced early; the dramatis personae should not be cluttered unduly with butlers, maids, chauffeurs, footmen, and other little-used human impedimenta; too much description of drawing rooms, hotel lobbies, estate grounds, or whatever would distract from the unfolding plot—it was the action itself that counted. She quickly perfected the use of the casual or innocent remark that was designed to be misleading.

In addition to tight plotting, Dame Agatha also early developed an economy and deftness of description which were outstanding. In a short paragraph, or even a few words, she could limn an upstairs maid or a solicitor or a duke so as to make us feel that we saw him or her personally with all the figurative warts and pimples standing out and emotions flitting across faces in very realistic fashion.

In view of the sheer volume of Dame Agatha's writing, it was of course inevitable that occasional mistakes and inconsistencies crept in here and there. It happens in the best of detective families and the great wonder is that there are so few of them in the Christie books. Vincent Starrett in *The Private Life of Sherlock Holmes* details how often at fault Dr. Watson is with the chronology of cases of his hero Holmes. Apparently the only Christie chronological blunder of consequence (and we can't say it wasn't intentional) makes the Beresford's son, born in 1929 or 1930, old enough to become an R.A.F. lieutenant at the beginning of World War II.

At the risk of seeming picky, a few other inconsistencies may be pointed out. On the first page of "The Case of the City Clerk" the client is "a man of forty-five," but he apparently ages rapidly; in the next page: "I'm forty-eight." Parker Pyne's first name is Christopher, but in "Have You Got Everything You Want?" his pigskin bag is marked "J. Parker Pyne." Poirot's valet is at times George, at other times he is Gallicized to Georges.

Her kinds of stories.

Christie was given to "family type murders," as it were. "I specialize in murders of quiet, domestic interest," she told interviewer Nigel Dennis in 1956. "Give me a nice deadly phial to play with and I am happy." This meant that in current film classification terms most of her stories would be rated G—they are suitable for the entire family and not even Parental Guidance is necessary. She had a total incapacity for offending. Her murders were raised to a level of calm speculation and cool logic.

Normally, violence and bloodshed were held to a minimum. One is reminded, by way of contrast, of an episode years ago in the "I Love Lucy" television series. The zany and delightful Lucille Ball was telling of three detective stories she had been reading. She gave the lurid titles of two of them and added with a happy shudder, "The third one was called *Gore.*" Gore is usually in short supply in Dame Agatha's stories. True, in *Hercule Poirot's Christmas* the blood flowed more plentifully, but that was atypical and the dedication, to a brother-in-law, told why: "...You complained that my murders were getting too refined—anemic, in fact! You yearned for a 'good violent murder with lots of blood.' A murder where there was no doubt about its being murder! So this is your special story—written for you. I hope it may please...."

A convenient but partially unsatisfactory and certainly arbitrary line of demarcation to draw among the Christie stories is to say that certain ones are tales of detection in its most orthodox form and others are mystery stories. The difficulty lies in the fact that so many stories, by numerous writers, are combinations of styles and formats and are not wholly this or purely that. The core of Dame Agatha's writing is of detective stories in the classic tradition: the presentation of a puzzle and then its solution. The reader is challenged to find the correct explanation before the author gives it to him in the closing pages of the book. By the 1930s the Christie books were mostly following this path; certain of the earlier ones had ventured into byways that partially departed from it.

Some of the novels and short stories are largely if not wholly tales of mystery or suspense. *Endless Night* is a case in point; *The Pale Horse* and *By the Pricking of My Thumbs* can, in greater or lesser degree, be so classified.

Then there are the spy stories. *The Secret Adversary, The Man in the Brown Suit, N or M?,* and *Destination Unknown* are of that ilk, as are some of the stories in *Partners in Crime.* A problem with such stories, most obvious with *N or M?,* is that they tend to be set in a time context that seems an invitation to patness. International intrigue is a closely related category. Probably the best example among the Christie stories is *The Big Four,* but *Destination Unknown, They Came to Baghdad,* and *Passenger to Frankfurt* could also be put in this basket. The intrigue stories are by no means the best Christie.

Of a quite different sort are the novels hung on the pegs of nursery rhymes, to which the author had a long-standing addiction. The stories themselves (some are short stories) vary greatly in their subject matter, plotting, locales, etc.— and in that respect that cannot be thought of as a "class"— but they all use the device of tying in to nursery rhymes.

The first of them was *Ten Little Niggers,* a British adaptation, considerably modified, of an American nursery rhyme going back to Civil War days and using "Indians" rather than "Niggers" as the unfortunate subjects of the rhyme. The novel was first published in England in 1939. When published in New York the following year, the title was, for obvious reasons, changed to *And Then There Were None.* Following World War II, a considerable migration of Negroes took place from British Caribbean colonies to England, and when an adaptation of *Ten Little Niggers* was presented in Brimingham, England, in early October, 1966, a protest demonstration was staged by Negroes. They had, since the original publication of the book with its objectionable title, become an audible minority in England. (One wonders whether, if the American Indian Movement becomes a more assertive group, the American paperback publisher of *Ten Little Indians* will have to arrange a title mutation.)

One, Two, Buckle My Shoe was published in 1940. It faithfully followed the rhyming couplets of numbers up to 20 when Poirot found his plate empty. *Five Little Pigs* came in 1943. Five chapters of interviews by Poirot provide the link with the rhyme of the pigs, but otherwise the connection is rather tenuous. The crooked man and the curious collection he assembled in *Crooked House* gave rise to another of the "rhyme novels," dated 1949. The Clan Leonides, central characters in the story (which the author regarded as one of her favorites), provided as varied a group as the crooked man, the crooked cat, and the crooked mouse.

The three blind mice who suffered caudal loss at the hands of the farmer's wife provided the peg for a long "short story," which became much more famous as a play; as such it will be considered elsewhere. The rhyme adds a highly suspenseful element to both the story and the play. The play is of course identical in title to the one performed by the Prince's actors in Act III, scene 2 of *Hamlet.*

"Sing a Song of Sixpence" gets a good workout from Dame Agatha. The rhyme forms the springboard not only for the short story of the same title, but also for another,

"Four and Twenty Blackbirds," and the Marple novel, *A Pocket Full of Rye.* It is in the novel that the theme of the rhyme is most faithfully exploited, but the tie-in in the two short stories is cleverly used. The mouse that ran up the clock was immortalized by the author in *Hickory, Dickory, Dock.* Barzun and Taylor damn it with no praise at all, but many would disagree with them. An early story pinned to a rhyme, but not included between book covers until *The Regatta Mystery,* was "How Does Your Garden Grow?," with the cockle shells metamorphosed at the climax into oyster shells.

Stories with a basis of fantasy form a well-marked class of the Christie shorts. Those in *The Hound of Death* all fall in this category; they include "Witness for the Prosecution," made over into a remarkably successful play. *The Hound of Death* stories miss by varying margins being classifiable as science fiction, a form of writing Christie admitted liking, but they miss it only narrowly in some cases. The Quin stories have a skillfully concocted base of fantasy revolving especially around the mystical, almost mythical figure of Harley Quin himself. Dame Agatha once said that she considered the "long short," "Dead Man's Mirror"—not necessarily a fantasy though presumably related— her best mystery story, but many would not place it in such a category.

The author had several of her characters playing golf, including "Bobby Jones" (not *the* Bobby Jones) in *Why Didn't They Ask Evans?,* but in general she eschewed sports in her stories. However, indoor games proved useful in two instances. Two are too few to establish a class, but they are worth noting. Chess is the open sesame in the chapter "A Chess Problem" in *The Big Four.* Poirot fails to keep the Ruy Lopez from being fatal but, *voilà!,* he does learn a bit more about the psychology of Number Four. *Cards on the Table* is built wholly around a game of bridge, of which Christie proved herself a mistress.

How and where to commit a murder in 10 easy lessons.

Detective and mystery writers are faced with an almost infinite variety of crimes their villains—or heroes, or just anyone—can commit. But murder is by all odds the favorite. The index to the encyclopedic Barzun-Taylor *Catalogue of*

Crime is not exhaustive, but it includes more than 250 entries beginning with the word "Murder." The choice of methods appears endless. Some writers seem, or have in the past seemed, to strive for the ultimate in grotesquerie.

Christie, too, was partial to murder. Had her crimes been real, she would long ago have subjected herself to many consecutive life sentences in Old Bailey to confinement in durance vile. But, occurring only on paper as they did, she was never dragged away in chains to any dank dungeon; instead, she received the acclaim of a grateful world. Her murders were plausible. Not for her a stabbing with a sharpened icicle which, melting in the victim's body, left no trace or fingerprints. Not for her the laying of a curse which in the face of all medical science would bring the miserable creature to an inevitable wasting death.

Poisons were in. Christie made good use of her two tours of wartime duty in hospitals and dispensaries. Although in her murderous methods she employed shots with a pistol, forceful drowning, strangling which simulated suicide, a dislodged boulder, stabbing with an arrow and with a stiletto, an induced fall from a horse, sandbagging and coshing, knifing, and other lethal means, her chief reliance was upon poison. Her alternatives in this respect showed great variety, depending on the sort of symptoms and circumstances she wanted to present to her bamboozled public. One time it would be strychnine; another, arsenic (passe now, but so convenient an ingredient of weed sprays; and remember that the author was an expert gardener). An ingenious device (thwarted) that she used in one short story was a delicate and artistic glass bulb filled with poison gas which was exploded by a high, powerful tenor note coming over the radio; this probably came as near the implausible as anything the author employed.

In another case it was a strophanthin injection; in another, potassium cyanide (that will do it in a hurry, of course); in yet another, pilocarpine (pile o' carp, get it?); in still another, digitalin. It might be taxine or choloral or nicotinic acid. The fatal overdoses of tranquilizers and of sleeping pills became almost trite—fortunately they were not often used. It would not have been as lucrative, but the author could undoubtedly have doubled in brass, if she had wished, as a pharmacologist.

Soon after her death, Dame Agatha was inadvertently

involved in a true-life story that dramatically saved a life. A dying year-and-a-half-old child had been flown to a London hospital from the oil-rich sheikdom of Qatar on the Persian Gulf in a last-ditch attempt to save her from inevitable death from a wasting disease. London specialists were unable to diagnose the ailment. Nurse Marsha Maitland was on duty at the child's bedside and, unable to do anything to relieve her deteriorating condition, was passing the time by reading Christie's *The Pale Horse*. In that novel thallic poisoning was the villain in a series of murders. Its most striking manifestation was a wholesale loss of hair. The hospitalized girl, too, was losing her hair rapidly. Could thallium be involved?

Nurse Maitland at once called the attention of the specialists to the parallelism of symptoms, fictional and true, and they, at wit's end, immediatley had laboratory tests made for thallic poisoning. The report: the child's body contained more than ten times the allowable maximum of the toxic substance. Now on the right track, they could begin appropriate therapy, and within three weeks the child showed remarkable improvement. It was simultaneously determined that thallium salts were a common ingredient of pesticides used in the girl's home area. Four months later the girl could be returned to her home in Qatar.

"Thallium is so rare," the British pediatrician-in-charge later commented, "that no one in this country would think of testing for it." Pharmacologist Agatha Christie had posthumously saved a life (cf. *Washington Post,* June 24, 1977).

Where was all this slaughter committed? If a center of gravity for the butchery could be found, it probably would be in an English manor house. The author, after all, was very much at home in upper middle-class milieus and what could be more natural than to set various of her murders there? *The Body in the Library* is a good example. (Its opening, a scatty conversation between Mrs. Dolly Bantry and her husband while he is still trying to waken in the morning, is, as Nigel Bruce quotes the author, "The best opening I ever wrote.") *Dead Man's Folly,* "Dead Man's Mirror" (a long short story), *The Mirror Crack'd, The Mysterious Affair at Styles,* two of the Battle books, *Chimneys* and *Seven Dials,* and others were among those that importantly involve country houses or their grounds.

"The one thing that infuriates me," the author confessed to interviewer Francis Wyndham some years ago, "is when people complain that I always set my books in country houses. You *have* to be concerned with a house, with where people *live....* It must be a background that people will recognize.... A country house is obviously the best."

Then there are the stories introducing trains in one way or another. (As she admits in her autobiography, Christie had a lifelong love affair with train transportation.) The most important train stories, in order, are *Murder on the Orient Express* and *The Mystery of the Blue Train,* although the author told an interviewer in 1966 that *Blue Train* "was easily the worst book I ever wrote...I hate it." But trains are found in the *mise en scène* in other stories too: *The A.B.C. Murders, Murder Is Easy, The 4:50 from Paddington, Passenger to Frankfurt,* and the short stories, "The Girl in the Train" and "The Plymouth Express." A fellow Christiephile has pointed out a curious anomaly with regard to Christie trains. In at least two of her stories the author mentions mythical villages or towns whose approximate distance apart can be deduced from the context. The time given the trains to cover the distance would imply a speed of two or three miles an hour—and not even the Long Island commuter trains into New York City (and certainly not British trains) could go that slowly.

Transportation by air is the locale in *Death in the Air.* A substantial part of *The Man in the Brown Suit* takes place on board ship. Bus transportation is central to the development of *Nemesis.*

Hotels do not get much of Christie's attention. Two notable exceptions are the Marples *At Bertram's Hotel* and *A Caribbean Mystery,* set respectively in London and the West Indian island of St. Honoré (as with certain other of the author's locales, don't waste time looking for this island in a gazetteer).

The Middle East understandably provides the setting for a well-defined group of stories; the author, after all, made many trips to the area. Such stories include *Appointment with Death, Death Comes as the End* (a throwback of some 3,000 years), *Death on the Nile, Destination Unknown, Murder in Mesopotamia, They Came to Baghdad,* and various short stories; one should add, too, the recently published (but earlier written) play *Akhnaton.* Not only

Poirot, but also Parker Pyne gets to the Middle East.

English seaside resorts provide a setting in a number of stories including the novels *N or M?*, *Evil under the Sun*, and *Peril at End House*, as well as in several short stories.

A rather curious "negative locale" is the courtroom; that is, there are very few Christie stories set in courts, involving trials, or introducing extensive cross-examination. In this respect Dame Agatha is much in contrast with Erle Stanley Gardner, for example, whose detective stories are virtually all set in the courtroom. The explanation is undoubtedly that Gardner was an experienced lawyer but Christie was not. A notable exception to this lacuna in her settings is the well-known short story (made into an outstanding play), "The Witness for the Prosecution." Dame Agatha in her introduction to Peter Saunders's *The Mousetrap Man* recounted how she at first strongly demurred when the producer wanted her to make a play from her short story. It would involve a courtroom scene—and she just couldn't! Fortunately Saunders won the argument and the resulting play became perhaps the author's best.

Dame Agatha views the human comedy.

The base point from which the author started her career, and the premise to which she constantly adhered, was that she was a "family-type murderess." If film rating could be transferred to detective stories, virtually all of hers, as noted earlier, would be G, certainly no X stories, very few PG. Profanity played very little part in her stories (atypically, in "The Gate of Baghdad" she has a character say "goddamned"), obscenity even less so, scatology none whatever. She and Mickey Spillane, both best sellers, have nothing in common. It is a safe guess that the Spillane fans don't buy many Christies and vice versa. Literary realism, if equated with plausibility, usually characterized most of the Christie stories, but it is not the realism of a Dashiell Hammett or a Raymond Chandler.

Regarding the rough-tough school of detective-story writing, the author once told an interviewer, "I don't find it very interesting—all that seems to happen is, first one side bashes the other side, and then the other side bashes the first one."

Sex enters into her stories when appropriate, but it is not sex for the sake of sex. It is neither prurient nor sadistic. It is often tender, seldom romantic, never mushy. Her treatment of sex was of a piece with her handling of most of the human emotions. They are dealt with in a spirit of gentility and leisure characteristic of the atmosphere in which she matured. In a sense they are done in pastel colors rather than in the violent tones and revolutionary designs of modern art. That is not to say that they are tepid or anemic. She could write vigorously and her stories were often swift paced. But the puzzle's the thing. Subordinated to it must be any literary flourishes, any neat turning of a phrase, any moralizing.

Now this does not mean that the author's view of the passing show was not altered as the years went and the stories came. She was aware of changing styles in dress, in diversion, in language, in social relations and attitudes. The house decor, the menus, the attire, the reading habits, the street scenes, the office equipment and procedures, especially everything that characterized the world of the upper middle class, were faithfully depicted by Dame Agatha as one novel after another was published. They were fictional vignettes of contemporary life, manners, and mores, passing through the lenses of understanding eyes and recorded by a sympathetic pen (or typewriter keyboard). Later stories making use of much the same milieu reflected the changes. These often served as effectively—and much more entertainingly—as the carefully researched writing of a Mark Sullivan or some other social historian, British or American.

A leavening influence throughout the long Christie career was the light touch or even the sense of the comic that she often introduced. When she used it her literary photography of the passing scene became almost literally a depiction of the human comedy. Here again it was use of pastels. She strove for the chuckle rather than the guffaw.

The best illustration of the use of the light touch was the occasional presentation to us of Mrs. Ariadne Oliver, the highly successful producer of detective novels (she wrote forty-six of them). Mrs. Oliver is the perfect caricature of the woman detective story writer and one wonders how much Christie may have been looking in a figurative mirror when she wrote of her. Certainly she would have done it with tongue in cheek and a sparkle in her eyes; no better proof could be asked that she did not take herself too seriously.

Antic though Mrs. Oliver is, the author drew her with restraint and never sacrificed a minimum of plausibility. It is comedy rather than farce. She attempted nothing such as P.G. Wodehouse did in his delightful spoof, "Strychnine in the Soup."

More characteristic of the Christie light touch is the *joie de vivre* with which she endows Tommy and Tuppence Beresford. It is impossible to imagine the Beresfords being ponderous or pompous. Some readers may feel that Tommy and Tuppence don't take their sleuthing seriously enough, but those readers surely are a minority. Miss Marple, too, can be puckish at times, and Poirot with his lovable egotism admirably illustrates the author's touch. One of the most deft of Christie endings is in *Murder in Three Acts* when Mr. Satterthwaite remarks that he might accidentally have drunk the poisoned cocktail and Poirot solemnly replies, "There is an even more terrible possiblity.... It might have been me."

Plays and pictures.

The author thought the first of her plays "must have been *Black Coffee* in about 1927" (see her introduction to *The Mousetrap Man*). *Black Coffee* was produced in London in 1930, but was not published until 1934. It was an original play, not based on a previously written novel or short story. Her first *published* play was *Alibi* (1929), based on *The Murder of Roger Ackroyd*; it was also the first Christie play produced (London, 1928). The publisher of almost all her plays in both England and the United States has been the firm of Samuel French (London and New York). In the early years of her involvement with plays she let some of her books and short stories be dramatized by others or by herself in collaboration with others. But, she later said, "I didn't like most of the adaptations and decided in future I'd do the adapting myself." Not from 1949 until after her death was a dramatization done by anyone else.

Christie confessed that with her first successful experience with her own adaptation of a book for the stage she "tasted blood"—the playwright virus had infected her. Members of her family were not encouraging and urged her to "stick to books," but she enjoyed this ancillary preoccupation because of the interesting techniques involved. She quickly learned, for one thing, that the climax of a play must come at the very end; in a novel or short story the explanations and tying tegether could occupy several pages, but not in a play.

That first successful dramatization was her adaptation of *Ten Little Niggers*. A producer wanted to put it on but his financial backers were opposed. "Impossible," they said, "to have ten people dying on the stage—it would just make the audiences roar with laughter." But it was produced, was successful, and but for World War II would have run longer than the eight months it did.

The collaboration between Agatha Christie, author and playwright, and Peter Saunders, theatrical producer, was long and mutually satisfying and rewarding. It created a close friendship and reciprocal esteem. Comment on only two of their cooperative efforts must suffice. In reverse order of their stage production, they were *The Witness for the Prosecution* and *The Mousetrap*.

On a visit to the Mallowan home in Devonshire in 1952, Saunders began his campaign of persuasion about the stage possibilities of *Witness*. The author finally agreed to think about them. She reread the story several times, got progressively more excited about its possible staging, and finally wrote a first draft in about three weeks. The play was a tremendous success and had long runs in both England and the United States. The author received an unparalleled ovation at the close of the first London performance, and in 1971 Saunders wrote that "If I had to choose my supreme moment in my theatre life this was it...."

Basic "vital statistics" on *The Mousetrap* are given in a note in the Master Bibliography. The principal question, now that the play has passed its 10,000th London performance, is: What accounts for its longevity? Saunders admits that he can't give a complete answer. Undoubtedly longevity breeds longevity, but imaginative and continuing publicity is a factor, as is the endless stream of foreign visitors to London for whom tickets to the play are a "must." Certainly *The Mousetrap* is a theatrical phenomenon. Dame Agatha wrote in 1972 that three people especially had been lucky because of the play: herself, as the author of the longest-running production in stage history; producer Saunders, the "Mousetrap Man"; and the author's grandson, Mathew Pritchard, to whom she made over the play's proceeds at the beginning of its run (and who has reputedly become a millionaire from it).

The Christie experience with motion pictures was less satisfying. Her short stories and novels would seem to provide an endless supply of material for films, but movie moguls are often cavalier and what they have done to some of the Christie writing is well nigh incredible, so much so that the author became largely disenchanted with the medium. She commented in an interview some years ago that the only picture with which she had been really satisfied was *Witness for the Prosecution,* in which Charles Laughton starred. It may well be that *Murder on the Orient Express,* which was faithfully transferred to the screen and had a remarkable box-office success in both Britain and the United States, also won her approval.

In two Poirot stories, *Blood Will Tell* and *After the Funeral,* film companies went so far as to substitute Jane Marple for Poirot in making the pictures. Of a Marple film, *Murder Ahoy* (1964), with which Dame Agatha had no connection, she commented to an interviewer, "They wrote their own script for the last one—nothing to do with me at all. *Murder Ahoy* was one of the silliest things you ever saw! It got very bad reviews, I'm delighted to say."

The refilming of *Ten Little Indians* in 1965 changed the locale from an island of the Devon coast to the Swiss Alps "for," as Ordean Hagen puts it in *Who Done It?,* "reasons buried in the mind of the screen writer." A later, third version again changed the setting. Is it any wonder that the author lifted an eyebrow at film treatment of her stories?

As her critics and reviewers see her work.

In general, American critics have been kinder to the Christie books than have their English counterparts. Could it be that the English reviewers were more discerning—or simply more jaundiced? But not all of one group saw through dark glasses or all of the other through crystal clear lenses. Margery Allingham, herself a distinguished English author of detective stories, wrote in the *New York Times* in 1950, for instance, that "With her brilliant contemporary, Miss Dorothy Sayers, Agatha Christie has helped to mold a somewhat loose form into a concrete shape and to give it both life and a tradition. ... Agatha Christie has kept [the genre's] hair short and its feet on the ground, and of the two writers she is probably, in the purest sense of the term, the

more intellectual.... Her characters are Gluyas Williams
models.... Grief, horror, and fear are out of place in her
books; the puzzle is the thing." A more typical, though by no
means universal, English reaction was one in a *London
Times Literary Supplement* review: her "writing is
abominably careless...formula hopelessly out of date....
Her books can be gulped down like cream or invalid jelly."

The late Anthony Boucher, long the *New York Times*
detective-book reviewer, was a consistent and enthusiastic
Christie fan. In a review of *At Bertram's Hotel* he wrote in
1966: "I strongly suspect that future scholars of the simon-
pure detective novel will hold that its greatest
practitioner...has been Agatha Christie—not only for her
incomparable plot construction but for her extra-ordinary
ability to limn character and an era with so few (and such
skilled) strokes.... The book is a joy to read from beginning
to end, especiallly in its acute sensitivity to the contrasts
between this era and those of Miss Marple's youth."

In her later years reviewers began more or less delicately
to imply that her work was not up to its earlier level. Typical
was what A.J. Hubin had to say in the *New York Times* in
1970 about *Passenger to Frankfurt:* "She conjures up a
hidden master cause, projects us a few years hence, and
creates a band of elderly men to deal with what by then is an
international menace. Unfortunately, the whole mood stays
one pace removed from reality, and the efforts of the benign
dodderers verge on the silly."

Quite the most devastating of the Christiephobes was
the testy and egocentric Edmund Wilson who, confessing a
boyhood fascination with Sherlock Holmes, gave vent in
three *New Yorker* essays in 1944-45, as his arteries
hardened, to his dislike of virtually all detective-story
writers. (The essays were later reprinted in his *Classics and
Commercials: A Literary Chronicle of the Forties.*) The titles
are revealing: "Why Do People Read Detective Stories?,"
"Who Cares Who Killed Roger Ackroyd?," and "Mr. Holmes,
They Were the Footprints of a Gigantic Hound." One comes
away from reading the essays with the melancholy feeling
that Mr. Wilson was the raw recruit with whom everyone
else in the company was out of step. But the scales of
assessment by reviewers, by Christie's own confreres
writing in the genre, and of course by hundreds of millions of
readers tip the balance far, far against the choleric estimates

of the few Edmund Wilsons.

Casting back over the Christie novels, the present writer reluctantly undertook to pinpoint a quarter-hundred of "the best Christies." He began with ambitious criteria of selection but soon found that the criteria simply gathered bacteria; the only feasible question he could ask himself was: Which were the most interesting? That obviously made a selection wholly personal, perhaps irrational, and inevitably subjective. But, with their identifying Bibliography code numbers, here they are:

The Mysterious Affair at Styles, I:1; *The Murder on the Links,* I:2; *The Murder of Roger Ackroyd,* I:4; *Murder on the Orient Express,* I:9; *Death in the Air,* I:11; *The A.B.C. Murders,* I:12; *Death on the Nile,* I:16; *One, Two, Buckle My Shoe,* I:21, *Murder in Retrospect,* I:24; *The Hollow,* I:25; *Blood Will Tell,* I:31; *The Clocks,* I:39; *The Murder at the Vicarage,* II:1; *The Body in the Library,* II:3; *The Moving Finger,* II:4; *A Murder Is Announced,* II:5; *The 4:50 from Paddington,* II:8; *At Bertram's Hotel,* II:11; *The Secret Adversary,* III:1; *The Secret of Chimneys,* VI:1; *Murder is Easy,* VI:3; *The Pale Horse,* VIII:1; *Ten Little Niggers,* XI:4; *Crooked House,* XI:6; *Endless Night,* XI:9.

This brief study is not intended to be an exhaustive or profound essay in literary criticism. A few comments, however, may be permissible.

Viscount Bryce in his *Modern Democracies* wrote that "Man is in each country not what we may wish him to be, but what Nature and History have made him." With but little modification we may apply that to Christie and her writing. Some computer—heaven forbid—might be able to devise a perfect detective-story writer. The hundreds we have had, from Poe through Doyle to the present, have been human, subject to the influences of their respective times. So with Christie. She was a product of what Nature, i.e., her environment (national, local, and familial) and History, or the sum total of social inheritance to which she was heir, had made her.

World War I brought profound changes to her Britain, but not ones as basic as those coming from the holocaust of 1939-45. The inter-War period, 1919-39, was, roughly, the Golden Age of detective-story writing. And some literary historian writing, say, five centuries from now, may catalog an author: "Christie, Agatha, *floruit* 1920-40." There is more than coincidence in the congruence of those two sets of dates. Christie was preeminently the reflection of that Golden Age. The nature of detective stories changed, as did so many things in the war and immediate postwar years. The placidity of the Victorian and Edwardian period—a surface placidity, at any rate—was being disturbed by more vigorous social and economic currents and crosscurrents, but detective-story writing was altered chiefly by its greater sophistication rather than its increased realism.

Christie, like others in the field, almost wholly ignored the rumblings of economic and social—and political—change. Whether by intuition or canny analysis, probably the former, she realized what the public wanted in escape literature and provided it unfailingly. It is true that political roilings did in a few instances give rise to novels with a Communist or Nazi or other international intrigue as a base, but those are among her weakest books.

Agatha Christie eschewed almost entirely the gadgetry that many writers of detective and related kinds of fiction employ so widely. Ian Fleming and the fantastic contrivances that he had James Bond make and use gave us the best example. Some analysts of the genre argue that because the devices by which Bond achieved much of his derring-do are so quickly technologically outmoded that even contemporary early teen-agers think of the dashing Bond as old hat, Christie, spurning their use, is immune from the datedness that already has overtaken Fleming.

But carpers—and they need not be as extremist as the late Edmund Wilson—counter that in a subtler sense the confinement of many of the Christie stories to the milieu of the upper middle class which she knew so well threatens her stories with a literary archaism that could be as serious for her future reputation as the technological advances that seem to be eroding Fleming's credibility. Such critics point out that Britain is in great social flux, that the upper middle class does not hold the apparently impregnable position it enjoyed in Victorian days and indeed even up to World War II, and that the institutions of the nobility and even the monarchy are under occasional attack. Thus Christie's must inevitably be a setting sun rather than a stable one.

But this sad fate can be doubted, even denied. The cases of Christie and Fleming are not parallel. Fleming's ingenious gadgetry was mechanical, impersonal. What

Christie used as a comparable base was the personalities, the emotions, and the general intangibles she found in the social world she knew so well. These things, it may well be argued, are even more lasting than the impersonal gadgetry of Bond. Are the Brontës, or Defoe, or even Shakespeare the less appreciated now because they wrote about humankind in generations long past? Christie, in her own genre, may well have as lasting an impact. It will come from her deftness of characterization, her skill in plotting, her ability to turn a neat phrase, in other words, from the elements that make any such writing lasting and readable.

Let us admit without quibble that she was a romantic. Not in a literal sense—there are no mushy love stories—but in her attachment to the gentility and the mores that she knew in her adolescence. She made little use of the meticulous examination of clues that made Sherlock Holmes so successful; rather, she relied on the exercise of the "little gray cells" by Poirot and the use of a skillful intuition based on homely analogies that Jane Marple employed so well. Much successful contemporary police investigative work is slogging drudgery or the diligent use of well-equipped forensic laboratories, but Christie gave no acknowledgement to such techniques. Perhaps it was because the formula she had so successfully applied for decades continued to be effective—though possibly with decreasing scintillation.

Agatha Christie was an intensely private person. No female eremite she—but she did, from childhood on, have inner intellectual resources and imagination which freed her from dependence on others for entertainment, for constant social intercourse as a way of avoiding boredom, for provision of models for plots and characters for her writing. Although shy and self-conscious through most of her life, she enjoyed dancing, group music, and conversations with small assemblages whose members she knew well. She disliked interviews and granted few of them. A list she once made up of her likes and dislikes is illuminating: "I don't like crowds, being jammed up against people, loud voices, noise, protracted talking, parties, and especially cocktail parties, cigarette smoke and smoking generally. ...I like sunshine, apples [move over, Ariadne Oliver], almost any kind of music, railway trains,...silence,...and going to the theatre" (*Autobiography*).

What explains the phenomenon that was Agatha Christie? It was probably the conjuncture of personal characteristics, the social milieu in which she was reared, and the nature of and changing currents in the literary scene at the time she was maturing. Certainly, she responded extraordinarily well to the impact of those factors. The result was one of the most prolific and remarkable writers of modern times.

L'envoi.

"What I'm writing is meant to be entertainment," the author told Francis Wyndham in 1966. And who can deny that she was supremely successful in attaining that objective? John Leonard wrote in the *New York Times* at the time of her death that "her books moved like trains of thought, each paragraph bearing its freight of fact, toward a surprising appointment or the derailment of expectation.... [Her books] were elegant as a balanced equation is elegant." Not all of those books will ring down through the ages as "great literature," but they have indeed provided to uncounted millions the entertainment she wished for—and that is by any measurement no small achievement. Edgar Allan Poe, Wilkie Collins, Conan Doyle, Gilbert Chesterton, and their fellows will welcome a worthy colleague to the Valhalla of detective story writers.

Selected Bibliography about Agatha Christie

Behre, Frank. *Studies in Agatha Christie's Writings.* Goteborg: Elanders Boktryskeri Aktiebolag, 1967. Baffling.

Christie, Agatha. *Agatha Christie: An Autobiography.* London: Collins, 1977; New York: Dodd, Mead, 1977. The definitive account of her life; nostalgic and introspective.

Dennis, Nigel. "Genteel Queen of Crime." New York: *Life,* 40. (May 14, 1956). A highly readable personal interview.

East, Andy. *The Agatha Christie Quizbook.* New York: Drake, 1975. A comprehensive set of questions and answers.

Feinman, Jeffrey. *The Mysterious World of Agatha Christie.* New York: Universal-Award House, 1975. A general review; occasional factual errors.

Keating, Henry R.F. (ed.). *Agatha Christie: First Lady of Crime.* New York: Holt, Rinehart and Winston, 1977. A collection of essays by a blue-ribbon panel of specialists, most of them English, giving analyses of and tributes to Christie's writing.

Murdoch, Derrick. *The Agatha Christie Mystery.* Toronto:

Pagurian Press, 1976. Extensive and useful biographical and analytical information.

Petschek, Willa. "Agatha Christie: The World's Most Mysterious Woman." New York: *McCall's Magazine,* 95 (Feb., 1969), 80, 129-30. A chatty, popular article.

Ramsey, Gordon C. *Agatha Christie: Mistress of Mystery.* New York: Dodd, Mead, 1967. A general discussion of Christie writing, with useful appendices.

"Perdurable Agatha." *New York Times Book Review,* Nov. 21, 1965, 2, 84. An appreciation.

Robyns, Gwen. *The Mystery of Agatha Christie.* Garden City, N.Y.: Doubleday, 1978. A biography, containing some nuggets of information but also numerous errors; in general it falls far short of the Christie *Autobiography* in factual material, readability, and overall usefulness.

Saunders, Peter. *The Mousetrap Man.* London: Collins, 1972. Ch. 8 and *passim.* By Dame Agatha's threatrical producer and close friend.

Tynan, Kathleen. *Agatha.* New York: Ballantine Books, 1978. A fictional account of Christie's disappearance in 1926 while suffering from amnesia; trivial.

Wyndham, Francis. "The Algegra of Agatha Christie." London: *Sunday Times Weekly Review.* Feb. 27, 1966. 25-26. A penetrating and informative interview.

Wynne, Nancy B. *An Agatha Christie Chronology.* New York: Ace Books, 1976. One- or two-page summaries of Christie books, plus appendices; occasional factual errors.

The Christie
Bureau of Detectives

Hercule Poirot

Some years ago a survey was made to determine the best known English-speaking fictional characters in the estimation of world audiences. Tarzan of the Apes led all the rest (and we shall refrain from drawing any conclusions about the nature or level of reader tastes). Sherlock Holmes of 221B Baker Street, London, ranked second. High on the list was a pompous, egotistical little Belgian who spent most of his adult life in England and who shared professions with the great Holmes. He was Hercule Poirot. Agatha Christie, who sponsored and chronicled him, was responsible for a character whose name had become a byword the world over.

There is confusion about the vital statistics of this famous man, who was second only to Sherlock Holmes as a fictional detective. Kenneth Macgowan (in *Sleuths,* 1931) thought Poirot was born about 1865. Julian Symons, writing in the *New York Times* on October 12, 1975, put his age at the time of his death "at roughly 120." If we assume that he retired from the Belgian police force at age 65, he would have had to have been born in 1839; but then he may have retired before age 65. The year of his death we do know definitely— 1975. The *New York Times* in reporting that death in a front-page news story on August 6, 1975, said simply that "His age was unknown."

Whether we accept Macgowan—that Poirot was about 110 when he died—or prefer the approximately 120-year age given him by Symons, Poirot was undeniably superannuated. Christie once confessed to an interviewer that had she realized when she introduced Poirot in 1920 how long he would be around, she would have made him a younger man. That would have avoided an anachronism— having a centenarian solve a baffling series of murders (at the cost of committing one himself despite his oft repeated credo that "I do not approve of murder.")

The circumstances of the writing of *Curtain,* the "last case" of Hercule Poirot, need brief recounting. As related earlier, this final exploit of Poirot was one of two books to which Dame Agatha turned her attention during the World War II London *blitz.* The manuscripts were intended for posthumous publication and it was only in 1975 that the author changed her mind and allowed publication of *Curtain* before her death, which followed only about three months later.

Given the time of writing, three decades before publication, *Curtain* obviously presented dilemmas. How old would Poirot be at the indeterminate time of presumed publication? What would the state of his health be at that time, where would he be living, and what would be the circumstances surrounding his involvement in a final case at so advanced an age? In the last pre-*Curtain* we have of Poirot (*Elephants Can Remember,* published 1972) Christie gives no information about his age. So—we'll just have to leave it at that: he was an old, old man when he died.

Nor do we know much about his early years. Born in Belgium, he of course spoke his native French fluently and frequently carried over its words and phrases into conversations in England and elsewhere. He was often mistaken for a Frenchman—an error he always corrected. His early attachment was not to the Walloon provinces of Belgium but rather to the country as a whole. He early joined the Belgian police force, and before his retirement in 1904 had become its chief (see "The Affair at the Victory Ball"). At the outbreak of World War I he was evacuated, after an injury, with a small group of other Belgians to the English country village of Styles St. Mary.

So far, so good—it seems like pure fiction. But we must remember that when Mrs. Christie's older sister challenged her in 1916 to write a plausible detective novel, a little group of Belgian wartime evacuees was living near Torquay in Devonshire. They numbered among them no retired policeman named Poirot, to be sure, but the circumstance, plus the great sympathy in which Belgians were held in England, was enough to give Mrs. Christie the basis for bringing Hercule Poirot into fictional being.

Poirot was then with us through thirty-three novels and fifty-four short stories before Dame Agatha's death in 1976. A very durable sleuth indeed. The third of a hundred novels are too many to list here, but they came along in a steady stream: five in the 1920s, twelve in the 1930s, six in the 1940s, five in the 1950s, three in the 1960s, and two in the 1970s. The decade of the '30s led all the others in number and perhaps in quality, although outstanding ones, for that matter, came before 1930 and after 1940. *Ackroyd* (1926) alone sold more than a million copies.

More than once the author admitted that she became tired of the famous Belgian. Nigel Bruce in his *Life* interview in 1956 asserted that Poirot bored "her to death and, but for the fact that he is such a moneymaker, she would have poisoned him long ago. 'I can't kill him, because if I did I'd only have to invent stories of what he did before he died, which is more difficult. However, I can put him into a wheelchair.'" And that is just what she did in *Curtain*. Willa Petschek quoted her as saying, "He's hardly the sort of private eye you'd hire today if you wanted a man to go and get tough with people, is he?"

We know very little indeed about Poirot's career before his transfer to England. Christie does, in "The Chocolate Box," relate one episode of his Belgian days—incidentally, it was the one failure he admitted to in his long career (almost as good a record as Gardner's Perry Mason could claim)— but in general the pre-England days are a blank.

We do, though, learn a great deal about Poirot's appearance and idiosyncrasies. Julain Symons put the former neatly in *Mortal Consequences:* it was "rather like that of Humpty Dumpty with a mustache." His head, at least, was egg-shaped, as we are often told. Usually it reflected a genial appearance, twinkling eyes, and a beaming smile, but his face could be stern and his manner authoritative when necessary. Poirot's principal facial feature was his enormous mustache, of which he was inordinately proud. He pointed its ends carefully (and used a mustache protector at night), pomaded it, as he did also his hair, and was desolate when steamy weather made it limp or droopy. In *The Big Four* he sacrificed it temporarily (and what a heart wrench that must have been!) when he invented a "twin brother," Achille, but of course it could grow back.

Also noteworthy were Poirot's eyes. Under stress of excitement or strong emotion of any kind they would turn green. To those who knew him well this chromatic aberration was proof positive that a climactic development was imminent.

Poirot was five feet four inches in height, surely no impressive, much less awe-inspiring, feature of his appearance. But what he lacked in stature he made up in dignity. He dressed immaculately; his impeccable couture made many people think him foppish and a dandy. He carried a large, old, turnip-faced watch but later exchanged it, probably reluctantly, for a wrist watch. His eccentricities extended even to what he drank. He would at times amuse, or even irritate, his English friends by asking, not for a good patriotic Scotch or stout, but for a tisane or a sirop de cassis.

His patent leather, pointed-toed shoes were always too small, but vanity would not let him wear a more comfortable kind or size. He scarcely ventured outdoors without a hat, and his phobia of catching a cold addicted him to overcoats, scarves, mufflers, and other apparel that most men would scorn. The same wariness of colds made him reluctant to expose himself to night air. A nightcap was standard bedtime wear. His hair he dyed black even into old age. He dreaded ocean travel, even across the Channel; the mere thought of *mal de mer* would send him into a blue funk.

Poirot's chief personality characteristic was undoubtedly his overweening—but lovable—egotism. On rare occasions he would present an appearance of modesty, but it was patently so forced and false that it fooled no one. Some of his own evaluations from one story or another: "Hercule Poirot...is of a cleverness quite exceptional;" "impossible to deceive Hercule Poirot;" "me, I know everything."

Probably as good an evaluation of that egotism as can be found is in a conversational exchange between him and his friend Hastings as recounted in "The Adventure of the 'Western Star;'"

"Console yourself, *mon ami,*" said Poirot, calming down. "All cannot be as Hercule Poirot! I know it well."

"You really have the best opinion of yourself of anyone I ever knew," I [Hastings] cried...

"What will you? When one is unique, one knows it...

"This street, it is not aristocratic, *mon ami*.... But there *is* a fashionable detective. *Oui,* my friend—it is true.... One says to another: '*Comment*? You have lost your gold pencil case? You must go to the little Belgian. He is too marvelous!...' And they arrive! in flocks, *mon ami*! With Problems of the most foolish!"

And in "The Mystery of the Baghdad Chest:"

"I am not an Anglo-Saxon. Why should I play the hypocrite? *Si, si,* that is what you do, all of you.... Me, I am not like that. The talents I possess—I would salute them in another. As it happens, in my own particular line, there is no one to touch me.... As it is, I admit freely and without the hypocrisy that I am a great man. I have the order, the method, and the psychology in an unusual degree. I am, in fact, Hercule Poirot! Why should I turn red and stammer and mutter into my chin that I am really very stupid? It would not be true."

Order and method were indeed Poirot's gods. At the time Poirot was brought into literary being, the chief and indeed almost the only detective model Mrs. Christie had was the great Sherlock Holmes. She imitated Sir Arthur Conan Doyle in some respects, in others she apparently by design departed widely from him. The copying included, most notably, the creation of a foil, friend, and assistant—Dr. Watson in the one case, Captain Arthur Hastings (of whom more later) in the other. There were other resemblances, but there were also differences. One was the incidental fact that Doyle wrote only four Sherlock Holmes *novels* as against the thirty-three that Christie penned on Poirot. More important were the differences in procedure that the two detectives followed.

Holmes could be systematic—he filed his cases in volume after volume of clippings and notes—but he could also be slovenly, and was often the despair of the good doctor with whom he shared an apratment. Slovenliness, however, was completely alien to Poirot. He was forever rearranging bric-a-brac to get it in a more orderly relationship, or straightening a picture that was an eighth of an inch out of vertical and horizontal alignment, or picking up a discarded match stub from the floor. Geometrical precision in furniture design, garden layouts, or the placing of books on library shelves always gladdened his heart.

Such differences extended as well to mental processes.

Holmes in pursuing his métier could be indolent while turning his powerful intellect to the examination of a case, and he often would be simultaneously smoking a pipe of strong tobacco or even opium, but his normal mode was intense activity in examining the minutiae of clues left in the room where the crime was committed, or in pursuing the escaping criminals in a power launch down the Thames, or in like frenetic action.

Not for Poirot such pointless expenditure of energy. Order and method! That meant, above all, once the facts of a case were fully in hand so far as known, use of *the little gray cells*. Reliance on the little gray cells became a fetish with Poirot and he was constantly admonishing Hastings—who, confronted with a case, was always wanting to be up and about, *doing something* (although he usually did not know quite what)—that a much quicker and surer path to a solution was to think it through, that is, to use the little gray cells. Poirot eschewed the retort and the Bunsen burner, the calipers and micrometer, the plaster of Paris for making footprint casts.

The cells of the brain were enough. Poirot also might smoke while using them, but it was always tiny Russian cigarettes that he used, and never, never would he have thought of keeping a supply of tobacco in the toe of a house slipper.

Holmes was a master of disguise. Poirot scoffed at the idea of a human bloodhound who assumed wonderful disguises and measured footprints. True, in *The Big Four* he did at the end disguise himself as his mythical twin brother but it was distinctly atypical. Given his appearance and mannerisms, disguises would not have been easy, and it was so much more effective to study the psychology of those he suspected of criminal involvement. Normally that study led him to the results he sought. "Always I am right," he concluded in *Cards on the Table*. "It is so invariable that it startles me." A person's psychology, correctly interpreted, could ever be relied on, Poirot maintained, to give the necessary clues to his behavior and actions.

Poirot remained a bachelor all his life. In "The Third-Floor Flat" he confessed to once having loved a beautiful young English girl but, alas! he discovered she couldn't cook, and for a gourmet like Poirot that ended any possibility of matrimony. Now, don't mistake his human reactions. He was in many respects old-fashioned but (in "The Mystery of the Spanish Chest") he admitted to a Latin liking for voluptuous curves in women, to seeing lush, highly colorful, and exotic women. But it was an esthetic, not a romantic, reaction.

He was particularly attracted to cases involving beautiful women, crimes of passion, jealousy, hatred, etc., but again it was an intellectual and not a sentimental interest. He was, indeed, fascinated by the Countess Vera Rossakoff, though probably not to the same degree that Sherlock Holmes was by Irene Adler (in "A Scandal in Bohemia").

Poirot's flair for the dramatic and the grandiose underlay his love of being mysterious and wanting to withhold his solutions of crimes until he could make virtually staged theatrical productions of them. He enjoyed making incomprehensible statements.

Poirot was essentially a loner but so richly developed did Christie make his personality and exploits that it was only natural, perhaps inevitable, that he should have an entourage of sorts. With no one did he develop a relationship such as that between Quin and Satterthwaite, but a number of people were in close enough association with him to add substantially to the three-dimensional picture the author gave us of her Number One detective.

Most important was Hastings, even though he did not appear in all the Poirot novels and short stories. Captain Arthur Hastings is the example par excellence of what some commentators on the genre have ungenerously called the "idiot friend." His model, of course, is Sherlock Holmes's Dr. Watson but he out-Watsons the Doyle army surgeon in almost every respect; Haycraft (in *Murder for Pleasure*) calls him "easily the stupidest of all modern Watsons." There are, of course, other "Watsons" in one degree or another. Several quickly come to mind: Vance's Francis F.X. Markham (Van Dine-Wright), Dr. Thorndyke's Polton (Freeman), Wolfe's Archie Goodwin (Stout). The grandfather of them all, though not involving a detective, was to be found in the association between Don Quixote and Sancho Panza.

Hastings was definitely born in 1885 and thus was twenty or more years younger than Poirot, to whom he remained *"mon cher ami"* until Poirot's death. He fought in World War I, was wounded in the Battle of the Somme, and was invalided out of the army as a consequence. As he related in *The Mysterious Affair at Styles,* he spent several months in a depressing convalescent home, and was then given a month's sick leave during which he fortuitously met an old friend who invited him for a visit at his country estate, Styles Court, in Essex. It was there that he met another old friend, Hercule Poirot, and began a long association with him.

Hastings had a good opinion of his own mental capacities. He was a man of action, rather impatient of Poirot's devotion the the little gray cells, and attracted to the spectacular and the romantic aspects of Poirot's cases. He was also susceptivel to pretty women, especially auburn-haired ones. He was quick to jump to conclusions—Poirot never did—and his analyses of Poirot's cases were invariably simplistic (and almost always wrong), but Poirot found him useful not only as a loyal friend but also as a sounding board to test his own hypotheses. He admitted (in *Ackroyd*) that Hastings, by then in Argentina, had often been helpful by stumbling onto the truth of a case unawares and thus putting Poirot on the right track.

Hastings often served as amanuensis and foil for Poirot, as Watson had for Holmes. Whether the narrator or not, Hastings appeared in most of the early Poirots. There is some evidence that the author tired of him, however, or began to doubt the effectiveness of the idiot-friend device. She ultimately banished him to an estate in Argentina, where so many Englishmen had become *estancieros,* and he was absent from most of the Poirot novels thereafter. In *Curtain,* however, she brought him back again, as an old man, to renew his affectionate association with the detective, fittingly at the same location, Styles, where it had begun. He had grown in years though not in perspicacity. His dog-like devotion to Poirot continued to the end and it fell to his lot to perform the last services in that confusing final case and wrap up the Poirot saga.

Quite a different friend and associate of Poirot's was the famous detective-story writer, Mrs. Ariadne Oliver. a prolific, though rather scatty author, she occasionally dazed Poirot by the vividness of her imagination. She appeared in seven of the Poirot novels, though the first time we meet her is in some of the Parker Pyne stories. She is addicted to munching on apples, running her hands wildly through her hair when in the throes of literary composition, *outré* and inharmonious changes of wearing apparel, and other eccentricities. She stars in *Dead Man's Folly.* Poirot found her amusing—and occasionally helpful in his probing of a case. Mrs. Oliver, as was also true of Jane Marple, may have been in some degree a reflection of Christie herself, but for the most part she was *sui generis,* introduced for purposes of comic relief.

James Japp was a professional, engaged in the same pursuits as Poirot, i.e., the tracking down of criminals. But whereas Poirot, after his removal to England, was engaged in private practice or consultation, Japp was one of the top inspectors at Scotland Yard. A ferret-faced sleuth, Japp was stolid, dogged, and umimaginative but highly intelligent, and Poirot had great respect for his ability. Perhaps an unconscious bond between them flowed from the fact that as an avocation Japp was an ardent botanist and Poirot had a continuing interest, long frustrated, in the raising and improving of vegetable marrows.

Japp professed to be scornful of Poirot's devotion to his little gray cells and at times he intimated that Poirot's solution of one case or another was due to luck, but the Belgian took such disparagement in good part and the two continued on affectionate terms. The inspector was typically British and certainly articulate, although occasionally he referred to the little detective as Moosior Poirot. That individual undoubtedly heard the mispronunciation with no more than a Gallic shrug; his punctilious courtesy would have precluded any protest, even to a friend.

Then there was Miss Felicity Lemon, Poirot's gem of a secretary. "Her general effect," the author said in one story, "was that of a lot of bones thrown together at random." Certainly unprepossessing, even ugly, she seemed to be all angles, a human machine, aged 48. She also worked for Parker Pyne, though undoubtedly only in intervals when Poirot was away from England. In her professional duties of typing, filing, sorting mail, etc., she almost never made a mistake—although, for good reason, she made three in one letter (in *Hickory, Dickory, Death*)—but she was at a loss when Poirot at rare intervals asked her opinion on non-factual matters.

She was a veritable encyclopedia of knowledge about *facts* (she could at once, for example, give her employer the address of Hell, the "in" night club so popular in London), but she thought speculation about matters of the mind a sheer waste of time that could be much better devoted to her lifelong project of devising a perfect filing system.

Then there was Goby, a little known but highly efficient private investigator occasionally employed by Poirot. Goby was so nondescript as to be virtually invisible. In developing his nondescriptness he somehow lost his first name; at least, the author never gave us one. In giving his meticulously detailed reports to Poirot, Mr. Goby would never look directly at the great detective. He would stare first at an andiron knob, then his gaze would shift to the valance over a window, then his eyes would turn to a light switch on a wall. But he invariably come through with the information Poirot needed for feeding his little gray cells.

Poirot liked his creature comforts, but it would be going much too far to think of him as a hedonist. His pleasure lay in exercising the little gray cells. The concentration necessary for that endeavor could be aided, he early found, by building multi-storied houses of playing cards or arranging geometrical designs from a child's building blocks. Those who saw him in such distractions often looked askance and wondered if he were quite all there, but Poirot did not care—it was simply an aid to cerebration.

Poirot maintained that he was a "good Catholic," but evidence of his religiosity is entirely lacking. His protestation of Catholicism did not keep him from telling white (or even gray) lies when they served his ends, or at least conveying a wrong impression with a seemingly innocuous remark or possibly no more than a gesture. He is perhaps the great master of misdirection in all detective writing.

Throughout his long career his delightfully fractured English remained, but as time passed Christie bettered his usuage of it; after all, he should have improved in familiarity with an adopted language in fifty-five years. A subtler explanation of the detective's improved use of English is of course plausible. His gaucheries with the language as revealed early in various novels serve the purpose of throwing Englishmen around him off their guard—after all, he's just a comical foreigner who can't speak English well and possibly understands it no better—and then when Poirot has thus sneakily learned things they probably did not realize they were revealing, his use and comprehension of English can quickly improve. Deviousness has its values.

Poirot never really conquered English and American slang. Miss Lemon's assertion that someone was not employing "elbow grease" left him baffled, as did the less common phrase "hairy at the heels" (i.e., deficient in breeding or manners). But for that matter the author herself was far from being completely at home with American slang. When she had her American characters use it liberally the conversations should have been vetted by someone familiar with American English.

Poirot had a sense of humor. A brief exchange from "Problem at Sea" will illustrate. The vain Mrs. Clapperton is trying to erase a decade or more from her age:

> "'You're so *alive*, Adeline,' they say to me. But really, M. Poirot, what would one *be* if one wasn't alive?
> "Dead," said Poirot.

Perhaps it was the sheer mass of writing about Poirot that unfortunately led to some duplication in the material. Two short stories, "The Adventure of the Christmas Pudding," I:36:a, and "The Theft of the Royal Ruby," I:37:c, are identical. The explanation is undoubtedly that one volume was published only in England and the other only in the United States, but it was an editorial slip-up that should have been avoided. A somewhat similar case is found in the pair of short stories, "The Mystery of the Baghdad Chest," I:20:b, and "The Mystery of the Spanish Chest," I:36:b. These two stories are not identical but are too similar to be offered as distinct.

Poirot almost inevitably invited comparison with that other great English-speaking detective, Sherlock Holmes. (Were we to include those who used other languages, Simenon's Inspector Maigret, for example, the picture obviously would become more complicated). Poirot of course has his devoted following, but it cannot be claimed that he has developed a cult. No organization exists, such as the Baker Street Irregulars, to apotheosize his memory, to explore minutely all phases of his life, to present essays or addresses examining or eulogizing aspects of his career. No magazine has been established such as the *Baker Street Journal*. No virtual careerists have come forward such as the late and able Vincent Starrett and Christopher Morely who gave their fealty to Holmes. No substantial corpus of writing exists about Poirot such as Holmes can claim (cf. Barzun and Taylor, *A Catalogue of Crime,* pp. 686-98). Why?

A few tentative answers may be given. Holmes was uncompromisingly British (remember how he decorated the wall of his Baker Street living room with a patriotic "V.R." marked out in bullet holes?) but Poirot, despite his long English-based career, remained essentially a foreigner. The foreignness was physical: he was a funny-looking little man, comic and even ridiculous, with an impossible mustache. Hastings once said that the first time people saw him they considered him a joke. But the foreignness was also mental: Poirot had a Gallic logic and an intellectual precision that even Holmes's keen mind could not top. Holmes had very little time or stomach for wit—music, preferably violin, was his outlet when sleuthing permitted—but Poirot's delicate wit was constantly surfacing.

All in all, Holmes added up to the stuff of living legends, of demigodlike proportions; Poirot did not. But Poirot made a much better next-door neighbor. Once you could discount or take in stride his eccentricities, he could seem to be "one of the boys." Personally modest, though professionally incredibly vain, he could overmatch Holmes's aloofness with his own friendliness.

Even though Dame Agatha became personally tired of Poirot, millions of followers did not and will not.

Jane Marple

The second of the Christie detectives—but Number One in her affections—was Miss Jane Marple, the First Citizen of St. Mary Mead, a small village in Radfordshire near London. Miss Marple's age was indeterminate, but she seemed perennially old. Lady Hazy (in *At Bertram's Hotel*) thought she "looks a hundred," but that was obvious exaggeration. Mrs. Dolly Bantry, a neighbor and friend of Miss Marple, was more moderate; she characterized her (in "The Blue Geranium") as "the typical old maid of fiction. Quite a dear, but hopelessly behind the times." Definitely she was in her seventies and eighties in the biographical episodes the author gave us.

We get much better acquainted with Miss Marple, and her home village, than we do with any other of the Christie detectives except, of course, Poirot. She made her debut between book covers in 1930 in *The Murder at the Vicarage,* II:1, although there had been earlier short stories. The additional novels are: *The Body in the Library,* II:3; *The Moving Finger,* II:4; *A Murder Is Announced,* II:5; *Murder with Mirrors,* II:6; *A Pocket Full of Rye,* II:7; *The 4:50 from Paddington,* II:8; *The Mirror Crack'd from Side to Side,* II:9; *A Caribbean Mystery,* II:10; *At Bertram's Hotel,* II:11; *Nemesis,* II:13; and *Sleeping Murder,* II:14. The last-mentioned novel had been promised for posthumous publication as the "final case" of Miss Marple. It was published, first in a two-part condensation in a United States magazine and then in book form in England and the United States, in 1976.

The Marple short stories are to be found primarily in *The Thirteen Problems,* II:2, and *13 Clues for Miss Marple,* II:12 (with some duplication between them). Some of the short stories are found in other collections, too, as noted in the **Short Story FINDER** at the end of this work. Marpleana is completed with one additional short story not included in either *Problems* or *Clues,* "Miss Marple Tells a Story," I:20:f.

Although not all the novels and short stories are set in St. Mary Mead, the reader of the Marple saga feels well acquainted with the village before completing the happy assignment of reading the dozen or so books. Fortunately the author includes a sketch map of the village in *Vicarage;* (published before the use of maps and diagrams became more or less passé among writers of detective fiction). For many years it was a typical small English country village; it was about twenty miles south of London and only twelve miles from the coast. Everyone knew everyone else; one person's business was everyone's business; and nothing ever seemed to happen (oh-oh! that's what *you* think, Naive Reader). People did a great deal of visiting by telephone, although of course it was not really proper to phone before 9:00 in the morning or after 9:30 at night.

After World War II the proliferation of public housing tended to change the face of St. Mary Mead and brought a considerable influx of new people only slowly absorbed by and known to the older residents. Miss Marple's house, fronting on the main street but set well back from it, faced northeast and adjoined Dr. Haydock's on one side and Miss Hartnell's on the other. Diagonally back of it was the vicarage.

Miss Marple herself was a prim, fluttery spinster. Christie's favorite adjective for her was "dithery." She reminded you of your grandmother or favorite aunt. She was somewhat above average height for a woman, always sat very erect, and completely fulfilled the Victorian stereotype of a "lady." She normally maintained an old-world, unruffled air but could on occasion become righteously indignant. As the climax approached in *A Caribbean Mystery,* she told Mr. Rafiel that she was Nemesis, and in the semi-sequel to *Caribbean,* titled *Nemesis,* she fully bore out that self-description.

This delightful and unpredictable spinster could be sweet-faced, sharp-eyed, and vinegar-tongued all at the same time. Sharp-eyed she was at all times; nothing escaped her. She could be knitting—it seemed she was always knitting (and the end product must have been tons of sweaters and baby coatees)—and yet no detail of the passing human drama, whether it were at Bertram's Hotel in busy London or on the hotel portico on placid St. Honoré in the Caribbean of simply on High Street in St. Mary Mead, escaped her constant observation.

She shared with Mr. Satterthwaite an inordinate interest in the doings of the actors in the human comedy, but where the snobbish Satterthwaite confined himself primarily to the rich and the well-born, Miss Marple was as interested in the oddities of behavior of her maid or the fishmonger's delivery boy as in those of anyone in the gentry or nobility. The semi-fiction of being a bird watcher excused her frequent employment of field glasses, useful for observing other things than just birds, but when, in later years, her keen eyes began to fail her she had to depend less on sight, more on insight.

Miss Marple was frail. She often required rest, but more than that she needed a crime or mystery into which she would get her teeth. Dr. Haydock, her bluff, shrewd, friendly neighbor, once told her when she was bored with the enforced rest while recuperating from an illness that the best therapy for her at that stage would be a nice nearby murder whose solution she could puzzle out; and—would you believe it?—it almost immediately occurred. (She quickly became well). A bout with pneumonia in later life prompted her very successful novelist nephew, Raymond West, to treat her to a recovery trip to the Caribbean—and murder promptly followed. In her eighties Miss Marple suffered from rheumatism in her back; to her great frustration Dr. Haydock banned her gardening. But there was no rheumatism in her mental processes. At one time (see "The Case of the Caretaker") when she was feeling depressed during an illness, she told herself, "I can't help feeling how much better it would have been if I had died. After all, I'm an old woman. Nobody wants me or cares about me." But that was when no murder was immediately pending or crying for solution.

Physically, Miss Marple was unimpressive. She had placid, innocent, china-blue eyes and snowy hair. It was a pink, crinkled face she displayed, usually with a benignant expression. Her manner was gentle and appealing but, as some of her more perceptive detective friends realized, she could be dangerous. She thought of herself at times as "ruthless." She claimed she expressed herself badly, and admittedly she did ramble at times and become incoherent. (She was, of course, not above doing so by design). She always wakened early and just after waking read in a devotional book for a time. Then she knitted, though in her later years her fingers were stiff and rheumatic for a time after arising. Her handwriting was spidery and spiky.

Miss Marple described herself (in *Nemesis*) as "a scatterbrained old tabby" but those who knew her best would immediately and completely reject that evaluation. But even her best friends were often nonplussed by her many *non sequiturs* and her seemingly irrelevant references, in the face of crime or mystery, to apparently unrelated village parallels; her friends often teased her about her propensity for analogy.

She could take it in good spirit, however; she had a saving sense of humor. When, for example, she received a legacy of £20,000 in the closing pages of *Nemesis* and rejected the bank manager's advice that she put it in a savings account so she would have something for a rainy day, she insisted on depositing it in a current account so that she could enjoy "a few things that one thought one would never have the money to enjoy.... The only thing I shall want for a rainy day," she told the banker a bit tartly but with an undoubted twinkle in her eyes, "will be my umbrella."

The rock-hard premise of Miss Marple's approach to life was her insistence that human nature was the same everywhere and that it never changed. The fabulously wealthy and remarkably shrewd Jason Rafiel, after only a few weeks' contact with her in the West Indies, accurately evaluated her talents, and in a letter she received posthumously from him a year later (in *Nemesis*) he told her that she had a natural flair for justice and hence a natural flair for crime. She admitted that she had "a suspicious mind" and made the point more fully (in *A Pocket Full of Rye*): "The great thing to avoid is having in any way a trustful mind.... Oh, yes, I always believe the worst. What is so sad is that one is usually justified in doing so." But at times she seemed a bit more charitable, as when she said (in "The Tuesday Night Club"), "So many people seem to me not to be either bad or good, but simply, you know, silly."

In *Nemesis* she confided to paper her own analysis of why murder was attracted to her as iron filings to a magnet: "Murders as reported in the press have never claimed my attention. I have never read books on criminology as a subject or really been interested in such a thing. No, it has just happened that I have found myself in the vicinity of murder rather more often than would seem normal. My attention has been directed to murders involving friends or acquaintances. These curious coincidences of connections with special subjects seem to happen to people in life... for no appreciable reason. I do not like to write it down, but it does appear that murders seem to happen in my vicinity."

The weekly meetings of the Tuesday Night Club were the channel by which much of Miss Marple's fame spread. It was a cozy coterie of the distinguished and the undistinguished meeting at Miss Marple's home for the purpose of recounting, in turn, tales of crime or suspense to whose solution the narrator was privy but which the others were required to guess or explain. Raymond West thought the setting in his aunt's parlor was especially appropriate: the solid Victorian furniture, the black beams across the ceiling, his Aunt Jane sitting in the tall, straight grandfather chair wearing "a black brocade dress, very much pinched in round the waist. Mechlin lace was arranged in a cascade down the front of the bodice. She had on black lace mittens, and a black lace cap...."

Patently the most noted of the regulars in the Club was

Miss Marple's old friend Sir Henry Clithering, well groomed, a man of the world, the retired Commissioner of Metropolitan Police. As a veteran of Scotland Yard, Sir Henry's credentials were impeccable, but the great weight he could throw around as an authority on crime was used only sparingly and he quickly came to give credit in full measure to the extraordinary deductive ability of Miss Marple. Indeed, he described her (in *The Body in the Library*) vividly: "an old lady with a sweet, placid, spinsterish face and a mind that has plumbed the depths of human iniquity and taken it as all in the day's work. Her name's Miss Marple." He went even further (in *The 4:50 from Paddington*): she was "just the finest detective God ever made."

There were others of distinction in the Club. The debonair Raymond West was of course always there. An occasional attendant was Jane Helier, the famous actress, sometimes called the most beautiful woman in England (a pity her brains didn't match that beauty). Joyce Lemprière, the well-known artist with the black hair and hazel-green eyes, became engaged to Raymond West, though she didn't finally marry him.

The Club included members of local standing if not distinction: Mr. Petherick, the solicitor; Dr. Pender, the elderly clergyman; Colonel Arthur and Mrs. Dolly Bantry, members of the nearby gentry.

Despite her protestations of not being really clever, Miss Marple's swift and sure penetration of the intricacies of the various puzzling stories usually dumfounded her fellow members, and contributed to Sir Henry's growing respect for her abilities. He passed the word along to former colleagues at the Yard. Inspector Neele told her (in *A Pocket Full of Rye*), "It seems you're fairly well known [at Scotland Yard]." Dermot Craddock, Sir Henry's godson and worthy professional heir, came to know Miss Marple well by association in several criminal cases; he and she developed the same mutual relations of affection and respect that "Aunt Jane" (as Craddock began to call her) enjoyed with Clithering. Craddock once commented (in *The Mirror Crack'd*) that "Miss Marple can contemplate murder or sudden death and indeed crime of all kinds with the utmost equanimity." She could be devious or even on occasion tell a white lie if it seemed warranted in her implacable pursuit of one she suspected of murder.

In contrast to the wide-ranging Poirot, Miss Marple was essentially an untraveled person. True, she did enjoy a bus tour through parts of the English countryside (*Nemesis*) and a dramatic few weeks in the West Indies (*Caribbean*), but otherwise her dim views of human nature were formed in the small world of St. Mary Mead and nearby villages, with occasional visits to the big though largely unprobed world of London. The Christie short stories in which Miss Marple plays a part feature, in some cases, other locales—the Canary Islands, a Cornish fishing village, the Devonshire coast, Dartmoor—but they are the scenes of stories narrated by Tuesday Night Club members, not places that Miss Marple visited.

In consequence, many of the same characters are in and out of the Marple tales. The Bantrys, Miss Hartnell, Colonel Melchett, Dr. Haydock, Julian and "Bunch" Harmon, Mrs. Price-Ridley, and others become old friends. A probable difficulty, it would seem, would confront a mystery-detective story writer, dealing with a narrowly circumscribed geographical area and the repeated introduction of the same characters, in refraining from the use of out-and-out sequels in novels or short stories. It is true that Christie in the Tommy and Tuppence collection, *Partners in Crime,* wrote several two-part stories, but they do not constitute true sequels. Nor did the author use the device in the books and stories making up the Marple evolution.

The nearest approach to it is found in the interesting relationship between *A Caribbean Mystery* and *Nemesis.* They are not true sequels; the settings in the two are entirely different and only one of the characters in the first novel is reintroduced in the second, and then only in a minor way. But the compelling figure of Jason Rafiel, so prominent in *Caribbean,* even though he is dead by the beginning of *Nemesis,* dominates the construction of the second novel. It is an interesting, even an intriguing, device.

With the assistance of the late Margaret Rutherford, Miss Marple broke into the movies in four films between 1961 and 1964. Margaret Rutherford as Margaret Rutherford was excellent—and Dame Agatha dedicated *The Mirror Crack'd* to her "in admiration." But Margaret Rutherford as Jane Marple left something to be desired. Great as the actress's talents undoubtedly were, by no taut stretch of the imagination could she be thought of as prim, fluffy, or dithery.

Jane Marple aged physically at about the rate we would expect. Her deductive talents, however, remained unimpaired. Too, she readjusted to the changing ways brought by the passing years. Had she been more familiar with Latin (she confessed to Rafiel in *Caribbean* that she was not) she might have exclaimed, "*O tempora! O mores!*", but she surely would have modified Cicero to make him read, "Other times, other manners." She was adaptable. In *The Mirror Crack'd* she was embarrassed by having to use the word "pregnant," but by the time of *Nemesis* she could use not only that word but also "rape" and mention the fact that an unrelated man and woman had slept together, all without batting an eyelash.

As various interviews with Christie record, she was fonder of Miss Marple than she was of Hercule Poirot. Jane Marple does not have the bravura of Poirot, but her insistent pursuit of justice, in her own modest way, does entwine her in our heartstrings. We were given that one additional adventure, published in 1976. After that she joined Poirot in that detectives' Valhalla where all brave sleuths go after they have fought the good fight.

Tommy and Tuppence Beresford

The Christie versatility in devising different sorts of detectives was again illustrated in the Tommy and Tuppence novels and short stories. Aside from the association of Harley Quin and Mr. Satterthwaite—and that is not a comparable case—the Christie detectives are always single sleuths. It is true, Poirot is occasionally assisted (?) by the inimitable Mrs. Ariadne Oliver—but who takes her seriously? Mr. Satterthwaite appears in one novel with Poirot, but the former is a virtual tyro at the feet of the master.

The author said that people were always suggesting that she write a story that would bring Poirot and Miss Marple into collaboration, but she set her face firmly against it. They continued to move in separate orbits to the regret, undoubtedly, of those many readers.

The conjunction, the collaboration, and the complementariness of Tommy and Tuppence Beresford is hence the more interesting. They are—or at least were—a *rouge et noire* couple; Tommy had had red hair and

Tuppence a vigorous, curling, black mop. As they grew older the red became sandy, the black developed streaks of gray. The contrast of colors seemed to betoken a sort of psychic affinity; O. Henry played on such an attraction in his *Cabbages and Kings.*

Perhaps the author's reluctance to have two main figures share the same stage might be explained by the difficulty inherent in equitably dividing the limelight between them. But the Beresfords' is a stage which they share fairly and enthusiastically. They are temperamentally different and they complement each other admirably. There is no jealousy—good-natured chaffing at times—but no hint of anything to suggest grudging or spiteful reactions toward each other. Rather, the sentiments are uniformly those of growing love for and confidence and pride in each other. Certainly Tommy and Tuppence speak each other's language far better than could Poirot and Miss Marple, fascinating though the potential interaction between the latter two might be could they but be brought together.

Another facet of the Beresford roles on the stage the author set for them is the *elan* with which they play their parts. They enjoy detecting, they enjoy people, they enjoy each other. Their approach to the job of sleuthing is that it is somewhat of a game and that they must take neither it nor themselves too seriously. Their accomplishments, indeed, assume in some instances the proportions of a great public service and earn them the discreet plaudits of a grateful government. But a phrenologist would undoubtedly write it off as the result of an outsize bump of curiosity, noticeable especially on the head of Tuppence but by no means absent from the skull of her husband.

The dash and verve of Tuppence, and to a lesser degree, that of Tommy, do not meet with universal approval. Barzun and Taylor (*A Catalogue of Crime*), for example, describe *Partners in Crime,* the only one of the Tommy-Tuppence books on which they comment, as "the only tolerable book about Tommy and Tuppence Beresford, because it is a spoof." But legions of Tommy-Tuppence fans will undoubtedly dissent. It is indeed true that the Beresfords are treated with a lighter touch than are other Christie detectives, but so what?—why must sleuths always be considered as humorless heavies or as pompous asses?

The five volumes in which the Beresfords "do their thing" are, sequentially, *The Secret Adversary,* III:1; *Partners in Crime,* III:2; *N or M?,* III:3; *By the Pricking of My Thumbs,* III:4; and *Postern of Fate,* III:5. They are chronologically logical: *Adversary,* set (and published) soon after World War I, sees the two as unmarried; Tuppence is still Miss Prudence Cowley, fifth daughter of Archdeacon Cowley of Little Missendell, Suffolk; they are in their early twenties. They had been childhood friends, had had a brief reacquaintance when Tuppence (the ubiquitous nickname is never explained) was a wartime hospital nurse and Tommy a wounded patient in the same hospital, and then had met again some time later when both had been "demobbed," were jobless, and were approaching being "stony" (broke).

Their analysis of a presumably bleak financial future led them, in a spirit of daring, to agree to form a joint venture for investigations under their private label of the Young Adventurers, Ltd. And adventures they did have, chiefly revolving around the mysterious Jane Finn. *Adversary* ends with Tommy and Tuppence, predictably, becoming engaged.

In *Partners in Crime* the engaging Beresfords, now six years married, proceed through a series of short stories, only slightly (but deftly) connected. Tuppence, at the beginning, is bored; she longs for excitement to happen. And— surprise!—it does happen. "Mr. Carter," an official high in Intelligence, comes back into the fast-paced events and enlists the services of Tommy and Tuppence to crack a ring of Communist infiltrators. In *Adversary* "Carter" had inferentially been a *nom de guerre* but in *Partners* it appears to be his real name. In pursuance of Carter's plan, Tommy becomes Theodore Blunt, head of a "front" investigative agency, Blunt's International Detectives, and Tuppence is metamorphosed into Miss Robinson, his efficient and inquisitive secretary.

They have a number of bona fide cases along the way, but never wander very far from their assignment for Intelligence. Toward the end Tuppence summarizes their record: "We've solved four baffling murder mysteries, rounded up [two] gangs of counterfeiters, ditto gang of smugglers...one jewel robbery, two escapes from violent death, one case of missing lady reducing her figure, one young girl befriended, an alibi successfully exploded, and, alas! one case where we made utter fools of ourselves."

In addition to Carter, another "staff assistant" who aids in the unfolding action is Albert (Batt), who in *Adversary* had been a melodrama-struck but very observant elevator boy enlisted in the sleuthing services of the Beresfords. By the time of *Partners* he has become a young man and is now their office boy, whose continuing fascination with sensational criminality leads him into all sorts of protean roles permitting self-dramatization.

One of the lightsome devices the author adopted for *Partners* was having Tommy and Tuppence imitate, for diversion in various episodes of their adventures, the behavior patterns of different famous fictional detectives. Thus they play at taking on the guise of Sherlock Holmes in one case, Freeman's Dr. John Evelyn Thorndyke in another, Chesterton's Father Brown, and even Hercule Poirot in the final one. It was this aspect, surely a harmless little whimsy, that favorably impressed Barzun and Taylor.

Partners ends with another domestic milestone being reached by the Beresfords: Tuppence announces to her husband that she is pregnant.

The rather curiously titled *N or M?* is set, and was published, in the early stages of World War II. The Beresford's twins, Derek and Deborah, are now old enough to be involved in the war, Deborah in a coding job and Derek in the R.A.F. But Tommy and Tuppence are left at home, twiddling their thumbs, so to speak: "It's always hard for people themselves to realize that they're getting middle-aged and past doing things," as Tommy bitterly puts it to his wife. The sometimes patronizing attitude of the children didn't help matters: "Daughters can be very trying," said Tuppence, "especially when they *will* be so kind to you." And Tommy agrees: "The way young Derek makes allowances for me is sometimes rather hard to bear. That 'poor old Dad' look in his eye." Tuppence concludes, "In fact, our children, although quite adorable, are also quite maddening."

Yes, the war seemed to find the elder Beresfords shelved. Mr. Carter—and it turns out now that he was in reality Lord Easthampton—is quite old, retired, and living in Scotland.

But then Mr. Grant comes to call. He is a friend of "Mr. Carter's," has also worked in Intelligence, and offers Tommy, to his dismay, a routine job filing papers in a government office in Scotland. During Tuppence's temporary absence from the room, Mr. Grant explains that what he really wants Tommy for is hush-hush work trying to identify and corral fifth-column agents who were seriously threatening the British war effort. It is so dangerous an assignment that even Tuppence must not be told what or where it is.

Tommy—as Mr. Meadowes—circuitously arrives at the small coastal village of Leahampton and takes up residence at the guest villa of Sans Souci. But Mr. Grant, and Tommy, had reckoned without Tuppence. Top secret though Tommy's work was to be, one of the first persons he meets at the Sans Souci is a fellow guest, "Mrs. Blenkensop"—in other words, Tuppence. Forthwith, she has to be admitted to the adventuring that follows.

Deborah and Derek continue to feel sorry for the humdrum lives their parents must be leading, but they needn't. The latters' adventures turn out to be far more exciting than coding and decoding or even flying in the Air Force.

Years more pass before we again meet the Beresfords. In fact, the author's dedication of *By the Pricking of My Thumbs* was "to the many readers. . . who write to me asking 'What has happened to Tommy and Tuppence? What are they doing now?'" Macbeth's witch's stinging *Thumbs* gives the answer. Tommy and Tuppence are now more sedate but they still have unquenched spirits and irrepressible bumps of curiosity.

Thumbs does not involve an Intelligence operation. Rather, it centers on the genteel senility and scattiness found in an old ladies' home. The senility takes one charming old lady over the edge, and Tuppence admits she is frightened, but the Beresford resourcefulness is never-failing.

The last of the Tommy-Tuppence novels, *Postern of Fate,* returns to the area of Intelligence work, really the Beresfords' forte. By now Tommy and Tuppence are both over seventy; the twin children are grown; Deborah is married, lives in Scotland, and is the mother of three; and an adopted daughter, Betty, who came to the Beresfords as the consequence of a tragedy in *N or M?,* is also grown and is engaged in anthropological research in Africa. The theme of *Postern* is again the threat of the enemy within. It all starts with a coded and ominous sentence Tuppence found in a sixty-year-old book: "Mary Jordan did not die naturally." From there on it progresses through a series of perilous

climaxes to a final and more pleasant one in which Tommy
and Tuppence receive a toast from high officials of an
appreciative government—and their valiant dog Hannibal
is dubbed a Count!

Postern is less tightly plotted than earlier Beresford
books. The first chapters tend to be diffuse and even
confusing. A suggestion of where the plot is heading is not to
be found before Chapter 12. But *Postern* too is eminently
readable.

The appearance and actions of Tommy and Tuppence
well fitted their personalities. Tommy was pleasantly ugly
and had a nondescript face. His slicked-back red hair, even
after it bleached to a sandy gray, gave rise to the affectionate
family nickname of Carrot Top. He thought slowly and
steadily, was sober and clear-headed, and was characterized
by a bulldog tenacity. Imagination was not a long suit with
him, although he could surprise even Tuppence in that
regard at times. Both he and Tuppence were extremely self-
confident.

Tuppence was not a beautiful girl, but her small face had
character and charm. She had a determined chin, gray eyes,
and black, bobbed hair. She was daring, quick-witted and
quick-learning (she had learned to read at age five),
imaginative, and unconventional. She admitted to worrying
her very conventional clergyman father who, she suspected,
had been secretly relieved when she left home for hospital
nursing at the beginning of World War I. An elfin, even a
gamin quality constantly crept out in her. In intuition and
cheery optimism she outdistanced her husband; in common
sense and caution she fell behind.

Tommy and Tuppence are unique among the Christie
detectives. They don't, fortunately, spoil their reflection by
introducing any element of broad comedy, but should one
fault them for bringing an Ariel touch to their detecting?
This reader votes *No*, never.

Parker Pyne

Parker Pyne—or, to add a first name which he almost
never used, Christopher Parker Pyne—like Harley Quin, is a
detective of only limited appearance in the thousands of
fascinating pages of Christieana (if that doesn't sound too
much like a citation to an outdated atlas). He is featured in
the dozen collected short stories in *Parker Pyne*

Investigates, IV:1, and in two other short stories, "The Regatta Mystery," I:20:a, and "Problem at Pollensa Bay," I:20:d.

Pyne is by no means an exotic figure; his is wholly and wholesomely British. For thirty-five years he worked in a government office compiling statistics. His imaginative mind saw in them more than just an endless succession of figures, figures, figures. They gradually revealed to him consistent patterns of human behavior which, by projection, could be made to suggest probable courses of future human action, just as the mass of them told how people had acted in the past. Out of such a discovery and its refinement in his analysis of it he built his intriguing post-retirement career which brought him many strange adventures, some dealing with crime itself some (the most interesting) with the manifold forms of human unhappiness and its resolution at Pyne's hands.

Parker Pyne needed no slick and sophisticated big-city advertising agency or any equally synthetic and plasticized television campaign to bring his talents to public attention. A "two-liner" which he ran repeatedly in the agony column of a large metropolitan newspaper easily sufficed. Day after day people were questioned, and then told:

**ARE YOU HAPPY? IF NOT, CONSULT MR.
PARKER PYNE, 17 RICHMOND STREET.**

Unhappiness, Pyne had concluded on the basis of his long association with statistics, could be classified under no more than five main heads, and once the cause of the malady was determined the cure should not be impossible, perhaps not even difficult. Thus reasoned this surrogate doctor, and his career proved his theories and therapy eminently successful.

If Pyne needed no elaborate suite of offices or large staff radiating an aura of activity and efficiency, he did at times find it necessary to call on aides. The most useful and frequently employed of these was Madeleine de Sara, used especially when a male client needed cheering, enticement— romantic hypnosis, in short. She was dark, languorous; had wonderful eyes with long, black lashes, a perfect complexion, a graceful, even a voluptuous, figure; and she dressed exquisitely. In other words, she was quite something. If necessary, Madeleine could appear as Dolores

Ramona (equally glamorous). In reality she was Maggie Sayers, a confirmed homebody rather than the seductive siren she played for stage director Pyne.

Her opposite number, less often called on by Pyne but available when women clients needed solace, compliments, or reassurance, was Claude Luttrell who, if the implications of the term were not so displeasing, could well have been described as a gigolo. He was about thirty years of age, graceful, debonair, handsome. He dressed perfectly and was an excellent dancer. He had dark, melancholy, romantic eyes. Most unhappy women might well respond to him with an increased respiration and pulse rate, their probably jealous husbands with a greater flow of the adrenalin of irritation if not downright anger.

Pyne himself, well beyond middle age (after all, he had been thirty-five years in his civil service job), was a big man, almost to be described as fat (though portly might have been a more generous adjective). He had large, well-cared-for hands. His bald head was of noble proportions. His long concern with statistics necessitated his use of strong glasses; behind them lay a pair of small, twinkling eyes. His voice was cheerful and matter-of-fact. In general he radiated a reassuring appearance which almost always invited confidence from even reluctant or skeptical visitors. He was a "specialist in unhappiness" and, though almost invariably of a hearty disposition, he never allowed himself to joke on professional matters; he was normally the soul of tact in discussing clients' problems with them. But he could on occasion be reserved and in his advice to patrons, stern, and a veritable "Dutch uncle."

He was recurrently and almost inevitably a spectator of many small human dramas and naturally he became an expert on human nature. Even the sight of no more than a person's back—how hunched, how rigid—could tell him if unhappiness were present, and perhaps why.

Pyne was no Sherlock Holmes, looking for microscopic scratches on the wall or traces of Trichinopoly cigar ash on the ground. Rather—though he did not employ the term—he shared with Poirot a considerable facility for using the "little gray cells." That, combined with his vast knowledge of human nature, enabled him to become the successful doctor he was in diagnosing his patients' unhappiness and in prescribing effectively for it. His occasional use of stage

props and dramatic fellow actors made him, in addition to
his pseudo-psychomedical role, something of a theatrical
entrepreneur. It added to his capacity for cures.

A major item in the Pyne armory of talents, however,
was that, although he was inclined to be bored by the
behavior of his own compatriots abroad, he himself was the
personification of British dependability and solidity. It
stood him in excellent stead.

Harley Quin

Easily the most unorthodox of the Christie "detectives"
is Harley Quin. He appears in a book, *The Mysterious Mr.
Quin,* V:1, a collection of twelve short stories, and in one
additional short story, "The Love Detectives," I:29:i. It is
difficult to prepare a biographical dossier on him because,
designedly, he remains "mysterious." He is in considerable
degree symbolic, though just what the symbolism points
toward is unclear. (Of course, if one pronounced his name,
instead of merely reading it on his calling card, it became—
harlequin.)

The collected short stories reflect another element of the
unconventional: Harley Quin shares top billing with Mr.
Satterthwaite. (Satterthwaite appears also in *Murder in
Three Acts,* I:10, where he in turn shares the stage with
Poirot.) So intertwined are the roles of Quin and
Satterthwaite in *Quin* that the central figure might almost
be considered a fusion, to be named Harley Satterquin or
perhaps Harley Quinthwaite. The two are symbiotic: each is
at his best when in the presence of and acted upon by the
other. This interaction is of course absent in *Murder in Three
Acts,* in which Quin plays no part; only once does
Satterthwaite make a casual reference to an inn, the Bells
and Motley, at which one of the Quin-Satterthwaite episodes
took place.

Harley Quin is an unattractive even if somewhat
nebulous individual. He is tall, slender, and dark. His voice
is quiet and level but compelling. His gaze is at times rather
sad and mocking, at other times saturnine. But his face is
mobile and can light up with a warm smile and frequently
does when the rapport with Mr. Satterthwaite is evident, as
it so often is.

Very little is known about Quin's background. He is
unusually reticent about himself. He obviously is a man of

some means and does a considerable amount of traveling, but just how, when, and where remains obscure. "I come and I go," was his unrevealing explanation to his friend on one occasion. That coming and going is a significant part of the essence of his mystery. He can almost materialize out of thin air, and when his role in a particular part of the drama is completed—presto! he vanishes. The only definite background feature of his career which emerges, and even that borders on the tenuous, is that he had earlier been a ballet dancer and had even performed professionally.

To Satterthwaite, Quin is catalytic: he has the happy capacity to stimulate and crystallize drama whenever he appears, even if those appearances are brief and sketchy. Quin, on the other hand, generously gives Satterthwaite the credit and maintains that his own role is simply that of placing the circumstances of some earlier crime or unresolved mystery in a new or more logical relationship to each other, thus permitting Satterthwaite to see events more clearly and to arrive by his own reasoning at the solution.

Satterthwaite thinks of Quin as a stage manager pulling puppet strings in a series of dramas, but the most that Quin confesses to is that he might have a knack for showing people things they had known all along, but could now see in a totally different light. It might have been a sort of Gaston-Alphonse relationship—each of the two is a thorough gentleman—but at any rate the confluence of the two minds results in a series of detections. It is not detective work in any conventional sense but rather a process of review and ratiocination.

Mr. Satterthwaite's appearance, personality, and behavior can be pictured with more assurance; he is by no means the mystical figure that Quin so often appears to be. One interesting, though incidental, aspect of his functioning in the Christie *dramatis personae* of major characters is that he moves through one novel and twelve short stories without acquiring a Christian name. He is always Mr. Satterthwaite or, to his peers who are on more intimate terms with him, simply Satterthwaite.

The absence of a given name in a sense reveals his personality. He is not a dominant or aggressive individual. Although he attends numerous house parties and other social functions—he is definitely gregarious—the newspaper accounts of such affairs invariably concluded the guest lists with "and Mr. Satterthwaite." But, though completely lacking in pushiness, he does get around. For one thing, he is well-to-do and can easily afford his penchant for travel, the arts, and intelligent and highly placed companionship. He drives a Rolls Royce (or rather, his chauffeur does), he has a beautifully furnished house on the Chelsea Embankment, he has a regular box reserved at the opera, he stays only at the best hostelries when traveling. He is always correct, fastidious.

Mr. Satterthwaite makes no bones about his age. In the Quin sequence of stories he aged seven years: he was 62 in the first story, 69 in the last. Unmarried and with no relatives about whom we hear, he occasionally feels in moments of self-pity that life has passed him by. In his youth he had had a tepid Victorian love affair but just at the moment when he was ready to confess his passion (passion?) to the lily maid she had told him that her heart belonged to another; he had held his tongue and put his own heart in cold storage. This episode remains a cherished memory to him, though his dilettantism and devotion to his own comfort undoubtedly make it less a reality than a figment of romantic nostalgia.

Satterthwaite ages gracefully, just as he lives graciously. He is a hedonist and an epicure, probably the author's best example of an aesthete. He is not physically impressive or even likely to be noticed in a group of any size. A small, bent, dried-up man with peering eyes, he seems rather elf-like on the whole. Some of his friends thought of him as a little, elderly, and not too active bird and his mincing steps do nothing to dispel the illusion. His personality strikes most people as negative. In talking with Harley Quin he gains in self-confidence, but with a Poirot or a positive personality like a Sir Charles Cartwright his normal diffidence almost automatically reasserts itself.

His affluence and tastes make the theater, the art gallery, the opera, and the spa Mr. Satterthwaite's normal milieu. Admittedly, he is more than a bit of a snob. He likes titled folk; personages appeal more to him than mere persons. He enjoys the company of women and indeed a womanish strain in his character often shows itself. He understands women and knows intuitively what they are thinking and what they will probably say. But his acquaintance is by no means limited to women. He knows

Everyone Who Counts. He knows, for instance, as most people did not, that "Anthony" Astor, the Playwright, is in reality a woman, Muriel Wills. He has acquaintances and friends—in the proper social and artistic circles, of course— all over England and on various parts of the Continent.

Mr. Satterthwaite likes good cooking, classical music, stimulating conversation. His year is more or less routine, even though reflecting much variety in detail. He regularly spends the period from the second Sunday in January to April on the Riviera; then he returns to London where he always attends the racing at Ascot; in early summer he goes back to the Continent, usually to Le Touquet or Deauville; shooting parties on the estate of friends occupy him in September and October (though he eschews any strenuous riding to hounds); then November and December are spent in London.

Satterthwaite's major characteristic is his inordinate interest in people—what they do and why, what they are thinking, who likes or dislikes whom, indeed, all aspects of the human comedy. He is observant and shrewd, a good listener and, when it falls to his lot to bring to life the atmosphere of a past situation, a good narrator. His gregariousness and gentle and sentimental Victorianism open many doors and many confidences to him. He is not an alter ego to Quin, but he does make a perfect foil for him.

Satterthwaite shows to better advantage in interaction with Mr. Quin than he does with Poirot, Cartwright, Egg Lytton Gore and others at Loomouth. He and Quin fit together intellectually like adjoining pieces in a jigsaw puzzle. In assaying the role of a more conventional detective, even though that role is essentially passive, he is inevitably overshadowed by Poirot, the complex Cartwright, and the ebullient Miss Lytton Gore.

Superintendent Battle

It is interesting that of all of Christie's major detectives, Superintendent Battle is the only one affiliated with that awesome institution, Scotland Yard. It is not that this preeminent exponent of the genre felt a lack of respect for the Yard and its detectives but rather, in all probability, that those in the various echelons of Scotland Yard service were bound by traditional canons of professional behavior which circumscribed how they could go about their work. Usually the author dealt with the Yard detectives with courtesy, though not often affection. It is true that Inspector Japp, though admittedly one of the more capable detectives working for Scotland Yard, is presented as a man largely lacking in imagination, but the Christie opinion of Japp (via Poirot) is certainly more generous than that held by Sherlock Holmes toward Gregson and Lestrade.

The great Poirot had of course been a member of the Belgian police force, but by the time we meet him he is in private practice. Poirot, of course, was held in high esteem by Japp and other professionals. The almost equally noted Miss Marple is a seemingly simple but actually astute small-town spinster. She too has respect for the official police and they fully reciprocate; in fact, Sir Henry Clithering, retired Commissioner of the Metropolitan Police (i.e., Scotland Yard) once told her, only half facetiously, that he would recommend that the Yard come to her for advice.

Tommy and Tuppence Beresford, Parker Pyne, and Colonel Race all do their detecting as a private matter. Only Inspector Narracott has official status and both he and it are relatively minor. Undoubtedly the reason why Poirot and Marple, Tommy and Tuppence, and, indeed, most of the outstanding sleuths given us by the great writers of detective stories move in non-official orbits is that they can thus reflect more *elan,* more flair and dash than the official and rule-bound detectives.

The eccentricities of a Poirot, the joy of living of a Tommy-Tuppence combination, the mysticism of a Quin could not be shown by an official detective, and Battle does not display them. He is stodgy and solid—"wooden" is a frequently used Christie adjective. He is a correct and proper detective but he *is* human; that is evidenced by the occasional sparkle in his eyes, by an even less frequent ghost of a smile (and at least once, a grin), and by his readiness to admit that he was following the wrong track at times.

Superintendent Battle is another of the Christie detectives who goes through life with but one name. At least, in the four books in which we meet him—*The Secret of Chimneys,* VI:1; *The Seven Dials Mystery,* VI:2; *Murder Is Easy,* VI:3; and *Toward Zero,* VI:4 (plus a minor appearance in *Cards on the Table*)—a patronymic and his official title are all we are offered. But he does have a family: a wife, Mary, and five children.

We meet the family (part of it) only in *Zero*. Mary Battle, a fond and sensitive mother, appears but briefly; the youngest daughter, Sylvia, not much more. A false accusation of petty pilfering levied against sixteen-year-old Sylvia in a private school near Maidstone brings a lachrymose reaction to Battle's wife, but her husband's calm assurance and confidence in his own ability to handle the problem—no loss of "cool" on his part—transmits itself to Mary and brings her a comfort she had fully lost. Her husband takes it in stride: "There was no expression visible on his face, for his face never did register any expression. It had the aspect of a face carved out of wood. It was solid and durable and, in some ways, impressive. Superintendent Battle had never suggested brilliance; he was, definitely, not a brilliant man, but he had some other quality, difficult to define, that was nevertheless forceful " (*Zero*).

The occasional twinkle in Battle's eyes was usually replaced by a look of shrewdness that, in itself, for those who made a habit of reading features and who had no cause to be suspicious or hostile, was trust-inspiring. The eyes and a large, handsome mustache were the most notable facial items. It was perhaps the shrewdness of eye (certainly not the mustache) that explained why the Superintendent was usually assigned to cases of a delicate political nature or those with political overtones or implications.

Battle is at his best in the first two of his exploits, those recounted in *Chimneys* and *Dials*. Chimneys was the country estate of Clement E.A. Brent, ninth Marquis of Caterham, and is the scene of both novels. Lord Caterham himself is not a central character in the murder mysteries, but the same cannot be said of his effervescent and hyperactive daughter, Lady Eileen ("Bundle") Brent. Bundle is a delightfully drawn character. She enters actively into the investigations accompanying both sets of crimes, the two series occurring four years apart (and the two books were actually published four years apart.)

On one occasion Bundle describes herself to the Superintendent as a "Nosy Parker," but Battle, though at times exasperated or even alarmed by the difficulties her activities cause the police, usually reacts with appreciation and admiration for her help. She maintains to the detective that she is not a fool, and he concurs: "No. Never knew a young lady who was less so " (*Dials*).

Battle had been known to boast that he had never been seen displaying emotion, but Bundle's forthrightness at times startles him and takes him aback. Ultimately, however, he gives her the accolade of accepting her as a lay colleague in some of his investigations.

Battle, the top deputy at the Yard, appears least prominently in *Murder Is Easy,* coming onto the scene, in fact, only in the last dozen pages or so. The one who does most of the detecting, though not always with infallible intelligence, is Luke Fitzwilliam, who has just returned to England after a career of many years as a police officer in the Mayang Straits area. He at first thinks that the melodramatic tale told him by a woolly-minded old lamb who had been a train partner on the ride to London is fantasy she has woven out of whole cloth. Surely there couldn't have been multiple murders in a quiet rural community with the intriguing name of Wychwood under Ashe.

Little bits of information which come his way arouse his policeman's suspicions, however, and, rather than taking his misgivings to Scotland Yard with no solid evidence, he decides to go to Wychwood under Ashe to carry on his own investigations. Some of his deductions might not inspire the greatest possible faith in the Mayang Straits police department, but on the whole he does well. Battle is in at the climax, but earlier action revolves around Fitzwilliam.

Superintendent Battle, though he is featured in four Christie novels (but no short stories), is not her most fascinating detective. The necessary limitation on his methods of operation and the fact that most official detectives are supposedly stereotyped as people of limited personality make it difficult to build him up into one of the vivid characters that most Christie sleuths become.

Colonel John Race

Colonel Race is one of the lesser central detectives in the Christie repertory. He appears in no short stories but is featured in two novels, *The Man in the Brown Suit,* VII:1, and *Sparkling Cyanide,* VII:2, and appears in an important way in the Poirot novels *Death on the Nile,* I:16, and *Cards on the Table,* I:14. If one wanted only matinee idols as sleuths, Race should have been front and center. He "was an out-of-door man, essentially of the empire builder type—

most of his life had been spent abroad. . . . Colonel Race was
not good at small talk and might indeed have posed as the
model of a strong silent man so beloved of an earlier
generation of novelists " (*Cyanide*).

Race is a tall, soldierly looking man (he had, indeed,
been a soldier—in military intelligence), erect and with a
purposeful stride. He is over sixty. He has dark, close-
cropped hair, although by the time of *Cyanide* it was
becoming iron-gray. As befits an out-of-doorsy man he is
sunburned or, at least, if the sunburn were not patently in
evidence, has a bronzed appearance. At times the face seems
sardonic.

Although, Race was not given to light or small talk, he is
a good conversationalist and an absorbing raconteur of his
travels and adventures, his big-game hunting and
explorations. But he is not an egoist. He claims to be harsh
and ruthless but his behavior, even gentle at times, appears
to belie that self-characterization. His personality is a strong
one and he is very attractive to women.

It just might be that an unconscious element in that
attractiveness is the fact that Race, in the event that Sir
Laurence Eardsley's son has actually been killed (as seemed
to be the case), would be the heir to Sir Laurence's vast
fortune. But one should not be cynical; Race's personality
was genuine and appealing without the possible glitter of
gold in the background.

Much of *Brown Suit* is ostensibly the narration of Anne
Beddingfeld, the daughter of an impecunious anthropologist
who dies almost at the beginning of the novel and leaves his
daughter to a career of writing and adventure which takes
her to Africa and more excitement than one could shake a
stick at. In places Anne's narrative is interspersed with
extracts from the diary of Sir Eustace Pedler, M.P., a man of
large enterprise and imagination. (Sir Eustace, incidentally,
is one of the very few Christie characters patterned after a
real person.) Colonel Race's role becomes intimately
intertwined with those of both Anne and Sir Eustace. In the
end he nobly gives up the girl and goes his lonely way toward
what Anne assumes can be only added greatness and
success.

Race's part in *Cyanide* is quite different. The setting is
entirely in England and a family involvement carries the
burden of the plot. Colonel Race has an important part in the

denouement, but more verve is added by the engaging Tony Browne. Race works in conjunction, too, with Inspector Kemp of New Scotland Yard. Kemp was a protege and former subordinate of Superintendent Battle, but whereas Battle had seemed carved from teak or oak, Kemp suggested a somewhat more exotic wood, perhaps mahogany or rosewood.

Race leaves the scene in *Cyanide* with a gleam in his eye (rather uncharacteristic of him), but then he had not had to face the bittersweet in this novel as he had in *Brown Suit*.

Mark Easterbrook

The Pale Horse, VIII:1, is the steed which carries Mark Easterbrook to his feats of detection, and a very good job indeed it does with it. The title of the novel, the only one in which Easterbrook is featured, is drawn, of course, from the reference in *Revelation* to "a pale horse: and his name that sat on him was Death." In the book The Pale Horse is a converted inn, many generations old, now inhabited by three women of dubious nature and curious personalities, locally suspected of strange goings on which supposedly border on the supernatural and savor of black magic.

Mark Easterbrook, the narrator of much of the story, is a scholarly individual, not old, not young, who is currently working on a book on certain aspects of Mogul architecture but who finds himself, as the story opens, going stale with the research. A late night visit to an espresso coffee bar makes him witness to a vicious fight between two girls. Later an old university friend, now a police surgeon, introduces him to a puzzle accompanying the seemingly motiveless murder of a kindly neighborhood priest. From then on Easterbrook's curiosity takes him on the long trail of unraveling that murder and others camouflaged as natural deaths. He has no elements of eccentricity about him and even a description perforce has to be scanty.

The professional activity accompanying the denouement is provided by Divisional Detective-Inspector Lejeune, a man of French Huguenot ancestry, sturdy, dark-haired, and gray-eyed. Lejeune's questioning of various of the participants in the drama is quiet and unemotional but is carried out with surprisingly graphic gestures and always with persistence.

Mrs. Ariadne Oliver, the delightfully muddled but

highly successful mystery story writer, is in and out of the
action at various times and provides her usual melodramatic
hypotheses, far-fetched or astute, concerning the solution. In
other Christies, Mrs. Oliver was often found in conjunction
with Poirot, but the little Belgian does not appear in *The Pale
Horse.*

Arthur Calgary

Ordeal by Innocence, IX:1, offers another instance of a
one-novel detective in the Christie repertory. Arthur Calgary
is strictly amateur as detectives go. By profession he was a
geophysicist, and it was simply his inescapable sense of
justice that turned him into a crusader demanding that the
long-obscured truth of the Argyle murder must be uncovered.

Calgary has just returned from a prolonged Antarctic
expedition. For two years he has been out of touch with
events in England. He discovers, by accident, that he
himself is the one individual—aside from the murderer—
who knows that Jack Argyle (Jacko to the family), the
enfant terrible son who had been accused of murdering his
mother in a fit of passion, is indeed innocent of the crime. Dr.
Calgary knows that Jack really did have an airtight alibi
that cleared him of guilt, but that ironic circumstances
prevented Calgary's revealing it at the time. Jack Argyle
had died in prison. Now came Dr. Calgary, reopening the
whole case, to the dismay of the Argyle household who all
sensed that if Jack, the logical suspect, had not done the foul
deed, it must have been one of themselves.

Why does Dr. Calgary reopen this can of poisonous
worms? Because "justice," "conscience," and "morality" are
such prominent words in his vocabulary. The truth must
come out and Calgary's persistent efforts are turned, almost
single-handedly, to that end. He is not a detective by
appearance or inclination. Although only thirty-eight, he
seems to the police simply a middle-aged, graying scientist,
slightly stooped, with a pedantic voice, a sensitive face, and
a thoughtful manner—"some sort of a professor, an absent-
minded bloke, maybe."

Well, the bloke is persistent in spite of the family's
aversion to having old psychic wounds reopened. He pursues
the case until the truth *is* discovered, maintaining that it
isn't only justice that matters it is also what happens to the
innocent.

Inspector Narracott

Detective Narracott—he seems to have no first name, at least for public consumption—stands out less clearly than most of the Christie sleuths. He appears in only one book, *The Sittaford Mystery (Murder at Hazelmoor),* X:1, and does not have the well-developed personality of a Poirot or a Miss Marple. He is police inspector at Exeter and is called in to deal with the case at Sittaford House near Exhampton. Narracott is an efficient and persistent officer with a logical mind and a keen attention to detail, a characteristic that spells success for him in many cases. He is a tall man with a quiet manner, rather far-away gray eyes, and a slow, soft Devonshire voice. He normally displays somewhat wooden features, as several of the Christie detectives do, but occasionally breaks out in a slow, Devonshire smile.

Bibliography

Compiling a complete listing (at least, it is fondly though perhaps vainly hoped it is complete) of the published writings of Agatha Christie is as complex a task as could be undertaken with regard to any contemporary author. Parts of her work, it is claimed, have been translated into "almost every modern language"—including Esperanto. Some of her detective stories (books) have been published under as many as four different titles, a few of the short stories under two. Certain of her books have been issued in condensed form as well as in full text. Some of the short stories have been expanded into full-dress novels, under the same or different titles, with the plots, locales, or characters modified either slightly or considerably. One book title serves also as the title of a quite unrelated short story. New editions and, especially, new printings have come out with great frequency, in both hardcover and paperback. Omnibus or anthology volumes have been numerous; some of these are entirely Christie, others include stories or books by a variety of authors.

But there are other complications: In addition to the vast array of detective or mystery stories, the kind that have made her name a household word in many countries, she wrote a handful of novels under the pseudonym of Mary Westmacott; many of her detective stories were dramatized, either by Christie herself or by others; she published half a century ago a volume of poems (and others later); she turned her foreign experiences in accompanying her husband, the distinguished archeologist Sir Max Mallowan, not only into some of her best detective stories but also into a non-fiction book, *Come, Tell Me How You Live;* she was an adviser in making of some of her detective stories into motion pictures.

Some explanation of the schema of the following Christie bibliography is hence desirable, even necessary.

1. It includes only publications in English, i.e., those issued either in Great Britain or the United States.

2. It emphasizes detective or mystery stories. It includes

stories (either books or short stories) contained in anthology volumes composed exclusively of Christie writings but omits those which share books with stories by other authors. Omnibus volumes with components all previously listed in this bibliography are bracketed and unnumbered but identified by boxed capital letters. Books or short stories are denoted by the numbers or letters (capital or lower-case) given them in this bibliography.

3. Only the first date of publication by a given firm is listed; later editions and printings by the same publisher are omitted. These initial dates of publication are listed chronologically. Changes of title from one publisher to another are given; an appendix lists such alternate titles. Except as otherwise noted, a first American title continues to be used by other American publishers and a first British title by other British publishers. Other pertinent information, such as abridgements or large-type editions, is entered in self-evident fashion.

4. Inasmuch as Agatha Christie's stories in most instances revolve around one or another key detective (and she made it an article of faith seldom to introduce her sleuths to one another), it has seemed desirable to classify her stories according to which detective(s) is (are) involved in the given story. Two of these detectives are exceedingly well known, the others less so. Hence, they are identified by Roman numerals as follows: I = **Hercule Poirot**; II = **Miss Jane Marple**; III = **the Beresfords, Tommy and Tuppence**; IV = **Parker Pyne**; V = **Harley Quin**; VI = **Superintendent Battle**; VII = **Colonel Race**; VIII = **Mark Easterbrook**; IX = **Arthur Calgary**; X = **Inspector Narracott**; stories without a central detective are entered under XI; and other kinds of writing, appropriately subclassified, under XII.

Arabic numerals, following the Roman numeral and listed chronologically by date of first publication, designate the specific book or collection of short stories featuring the given detective. Titles in anthologies, the component entries in which have all been previously listed, are not given separate Arabic numerals. Titles of short stories are designated by lower-case letters in the order in which they are printed in given collections of short stories, all of which are listed in an appendix. All-Christie anthologies featuring more than one of her sleuths are listed under the various detectives encountered.

5. Prior serializations of books, either in magazines or newspapers, are omitted, as are television and radio adaptations and several short stories published as separates.

Being informed of such guidelines, *caveat lector.* Let him especially remember, in using the bibliography or index, that I = **Poirot** and II = **Marple**. Happy hunting!

I. Hercule Poirot

1. *The Mysterious Affair at Styles.* London: Lane, 1920; New York: Dodd, Mead, 1927; New York: National Book, 1927; New York: Grosset and Dunlap, 1928; London: Penguin Books, 1935; New York: New Avon Library, 1945; London: Pan Books, 1954; New York: Bantam Books, 1961; London: Longmans, 1965; Boston: Hall, 1976 (large print).

2. *Murder on the Links.* New York: Dodd, Mead, 1923; London: Lane, 1923; London: Penguin Books, 1936; London: Transworld, 1954; New York: Dell, 1956; London: Pan Books, 1960; London: Hodden and Stoughton, 1968; Leicester, Eng.: Ulverscroft, 1977 (large print).

3. *Poirot Investigates.* London: Lane, 1924; New York: Dodd, Mead, 1925; New York: American Mercury, 1943; London: Pan Books, 1955; New York: Bantam Books, 1961. (All **Poirot**) a. "The Adventure of The Western Star," b. "The Tragedy at Marsdon Manor;" c. "The Adventure of the Cheap Flat;" d. "The Mystery of Hunter's Lodge;" e. "The Million Dollar Bond Robbery;" f. "The Adventure of the Egyptian Tomb;" g. "The Jewel Robbery at the Grand Metropolitan;" h. "The Kidnapped Prime Minister;" i. "The Disappearance of Mr. Davenheim;" j. "The Adventure of the Italian Nobleman;" k. "The Case of the Missing Will;" l. "The Veiled Lady" [omitted from British editions]; m. "The Lost Mine" [omitted from British editions]; n. "The Chocolate Box" [omitted from British editions]

4. *The Murder of Roger Ackroyd.* London: Collins, 1926; New York: Dodd, Mead, 1926; New York: Grosset and Dunlap, 1927; New York: Pocket Books, 1939; New York: Triangle Books, 1943; London: Penguin Book, 1948; London: Fontana Books, 1957; Leicester, Eng.: Ulverscroft, 1972 (large print).

5. *The Big Four.* London: Collins, 1927; New York: Dodd, Mead, 1927; London: Penguin Books, 1957; London: Pan Books, 1961; New York: Dell, 1965; London: Fontana Books, 1965; Leicester, Eng.: Ulverscroft, 1974 (large print).

6. *The Mystery of the Blue Train.* London: Collins, 1928; New York: Dodd, Mead, 1928; New York: Grosset and Dunlap, 1928; New York: Pocket Books, 1940; London: Penguin Books,

1948; London: Pan Books, 1954; London: Fontana Books, 1958; Leicester, Eng.: Ulverscroft, 1976 (large print).

[/A/ *Agatha Christie Omnibus.* London: Lane, 1931. (Includes: I:1; I:2; I:3)]

7. *Peril at End House.* New York: Dodd, Mead, 1932; London: Collins, 1932; New York: Modern Age Books, 1938; New York: Pocket Books, 1942; London: Penguin Books, 1948; London: Fontana Books, 1961; London: Pan Books, 1966.

[/B/ *The Agatha Christie Omnibus of Crime.* London: Collins, 1932. (Includes: X:1; VI:2; I:4)]

8. *Lord Edgware Dies.* London: Collins, 1933; New York: Dodd, Mead, 1933 (*13 at Dinner*); New York: Dell, 1944; London: Penguin Books, 1948; London: Fontana Books, 1954; Leicester, Eng.: Ulverscroft, 1970 (large print).

9. *Murder on the Orient Express.* London: Collins, 1934; New York: Dodd, Mead, 1934 [*Murder in the Calais Coach*]; New York: L.E. Spivak, 1934 (abridged); New York: Pocket Books, 1940; London: Penguin Books, 1948; London: Fontana Books, 1959; Leicester, Eng.: Ulverscroft, 1965 (large print).

10. *Murder in Three Acts.* New York: Dodd, Mead, 1934; London: Collins, 1935 [*Three-Act Tragedy*]; New York: New Avon Library, 1944; London: Fontana Books, 1957; New York: Popular Library, 1961; London: Pan Books, 1964; Leicester, Eng.: Ulverscroft, 1975 (large print).

11. *Death in the Air.* New York: Dodd, Mead, 1935; London: Collins, 1935 [*Death in the Clouds*]; New York: Triangle Books, 1939; New York: New Avon Library, 1946; London: Fontana Books, 1957; New York: Popular Library, 1961; London: Pan Books, 1964; Leicester, Eng.: Ulverscroft, 1967 (large print).

12. *The A.B.C. Murders.* London: Collins, 1936; New York: Dodd, Mead, 1936; New York: Pocket Books, 1941; Cleveland: World Publishing, 1945; London: Pan Books, 1958; London: Fontana Books, 1968.

13. *Murder in Mesopotamia.* London: Collins, 1936; New York: Dodd, Mead, 1936; New York: Dell, 1943; London: Pan Books, 1952; London: Penguin Books, 1955; London: Fontana Books, 1962; Leicester, Eng.: Ulverscroft, 1969 (large print).

[/C/ *Hercule Poirot, Master Detective.* New York: Dodd, Mead, 1936; New York: Grosset and Dunlap, 1937 [*Three Christie Crimes.* (Each book includes: I:4; I:9; I:8)]

14. *Cards on the Table.* London: Collins, 1936; New York: Grosset and Dunlap, 1936; New York: Dodd, Mead, 1937; London: Pan Books, 1951; New York: Dell, 1954; London: Fontana Books, 1957; Leicester, Eng.: Ulverscroft, 1969 (large print).

15. *Dumb Witness.* London: Collins, 1937; New York: Dodd, Mead, 1937 [*Poirot Loses a Client*]; New York: Collier, 1937; Cleveland: World Publishing, 1944; New York: New Avon Library, 1945; London: Pan Books, 1949; London: Fontana Books, 1958; New York: Dell, 1965; Leicester, Eng.: Ulverscroft, 1973 (large print).

16. *Death on the Nile.* London: Collins, 1937; New York: Dodd, Mead, 1938; New York: Grosset and Dunlap, 1939; London: Pan Books, 1949; London: Penguin Books, 1953; London: Fontana Books, 1960; New York: Bantam Books, 1963; Leicester, Eng.: Ulverscroft, 1972 (large print). [The short story with an identical title is unrelated to this novel.]

17. *Murder in the Mews.* London: Collins, 1937; New York: Dodd, Mead, 1937 [*Dead Man's Mirror*]; London: Oldham's Press, 1937; London: Pan Books, 1954; New York: Dell, 1958; London: Penguin Books, 1961; London: Fontana Books, 1964; Leicester, Eng.: Ulverscroft, 1971 (large print).

(All **Poirot**) a. "Murder in the Mews;" b. "The Incredible Theft" [omitted from *Dead Man's Mirror*]; c. "Dead Man's Mirror;" d. "Triangle at Rhodes."

[/D/ *The Perilous Journeys of Hercule Poirot.* New York: Dodd, Mead, 1937. (Includes: I:6; I:16; I:13)]

18. *Appointment with Death.* New York: Collier, 1937; London: Collins, 1938; New York: Dodd, Mead, 1938; New York: Grosset and Dunlap, 1938; London: Penguin Books, 1948; New York: Dell, 1952; London: Pan Books, 1957; London: Fontana Books, 1960; Leicester, Eng.: Ulverscroft, 1975 (large print).

19. *Hercule Poirot's Christmas.* London: Collins, 1938; New York: Dodd, Mead, 1938 [*Murder for Christmas*]; New York: Dell, 1939; New York: Grosset and Dunlap, 1940; New York: Books, Inc., 1944; New York: New Avon Library, 1947 [*A Holiday for Murder*]; London: Fontana Books, 1957; New York: Bantam Books, 1962; London: Pan Books, 1967.

20. *The Regatta Mystery.* New York: Dodd, Mead, 1939; New York: L.E. Spivak, 1939 (abridged); London: Vallancey Press, 1941; New York: Bantam Books, 1943 [*Poirot and the Regatta Mystery*]; New York: Dell, 1964.

a. "The Regatta Mystery" (**Pyne**); b. "The Mystery of the Baghdad Chest" (**Poirot**) [cf. "The Mystery of the Spanish Chest": I:36:b]; c. "How Does Your Garden Grow?" (**Poirot**); d. "Problem at Pollensa Bay" (**Pyne**); e. "Yellow Iris" (**Poirot**) [expanded into the novel *Sparkling Cyanide*: VII:2]; f. "Miss Marple Tells a Story" (**Marple**); g. "The Dream" (**Poirot**); h. "In a Glass Darkly" (none); i. "Problem at Sea" (**Poirot**).

21. *One, Two, Buckle My Shoe.* London: Collins, 1940; New

York: Dodd, Mead, 1941 [*The Patriotic Murders*]; New York: Grosset and Dunlap, 1941; New York: Dell, 1953 [*An Overdose of Death*]; London: Pan Books, 1956; London: Fontana Books, 1959; Leicester, Eng.: Ulverscroft, 1973 (large print).

22. *Sad Cypress.* London: Collins, 1940; New York: Dodd, Mead, 1940; New York: Collier, 1940; New York: Dell, 1945; London: Pan Books, 1954; London: Fontana Books, 1959; Leicester, Eng.: Ulverscroft, 1965 (large print).

23. *Evil under the Sun.* London: Collins, 1941; New York: Dodd, Mead, 1941; New York: Grosset and Dunlap, 1941; New York: Pocket Books, 1945; London: Fontana Books, 1957; London: Pan Books, 1963; Leicester, Eng.: Ulverscroft, 1971 (large print).

24. *Murder in Retrospect.* New York: Dodd, Mead, 1942; London: Collins, 1943 [*Five Little Pigs*]; New York: Dell, 1953; London: Pan Books, 1953; London: Fontana Books, 1959.

[/E/ *Triple Threat; Exploits of Three Famous Detectives: Hercule Poirot, Harley Quin, and Tuppence.* New York: Dodd, Mead, 1943; Cleveland: World Publishing, 1944 [*Crime Reader*]. (Each book includes: I:3; V:1; III:2)]

25. *The Hollow.* London: Collins, 1946; New York: Dodd, Mead, 1946 [*Murder after Hours*]; London: Pan Books, 1950; London: Pan Books, 1950; London: Fontana Books, 1951; New York: Dell, 1961; Leicester, Eng.: Ulverscroft, 1974 (large print).

[/F/ *Poirot Lends a Hand.* London and New York: Polybooks, 1946. (Includes: I:20:d; I;20:a; I:3:1)]

26. *The Labours of Hercules.* London: Collins, 1947; New York: Dodd, Mead, 1947; London: Penguin Books, 1953; New York: Dell, 1956; London: Fontana Books, 1961; London: Pan Books, 1971.

(All **Poirot**) a. "How It All Came About;" b. "The Nemean Lion;" c. "The Lernean Hydra;" d. "The Arcadian Deer;" e. "The Erymanthian Boar;" f. "The Augean Stables;" g. "The Stymphalean Birds;" h. "The Cretan Bull;" i. "The Horses of Diomedes;" j. "The Girdle of Hippolyta;" k. "The Flock of Geryon;" l. "The Apples of the Hesperides;" m. "The Capture of Cerberus."

27. *Taken at the Flood.* London: Collins, 1948; New York: Dodd, Mead, 1948 [*There Is a Tide*]; New York: Dell, 1955; London: Fontana Books, 1961; London: Pan Books, 1965; Leicester, Eng.: Ulverscroft, 1971 (large print).

28. *The Witness for the Prosecution.* New York: Dodd, Mead, 1948; New York: Dell, 1955; London: Fontana books, 1958.

a. "The Witness for the Prosecution" (none); b. "The Red Signal" (none); c. "The Fourth Man" (none); d. "S.O.S."

(none); e. "Where There's a Will" (none) [British title: "Wireless"]; f. "The Mystery of the Blue Jar" (none); g. "Philomel Cottage" (none); h. "Accident" (none); i. "The Second Gong" (**Poirot**) [expanded into the novel *Murder in the Mews:* I:17:a].

29. *Three Blind Mice.* New York: Dodd, Mead, 1950; New York: Dell, 1954 [*The Mousetrap*].

a. "Three Blind Mice" (none); b. "Strange Jest" (**Marple**); c. "Tape-Measure Murder" (**Marple**); d. "The Case of the Perfect Maid" (**Marple**); e. "The Case of the Caretaker" (**Marple**); f. "The Third-Floor Flat" (**Poirot**); g. "The Adventure of Johnny Waverly" (**Poirot**); h. "Four and Twenty Blackbirds" (**Poirot**); i. "The Love Detectives" (**Quin**).

30. *The Under Dog.* New York: Dodd, Mead, 1951; New York: Pocket Books, 1955; New York: Dell, 1965.

(All **Poirot**) a. "The Under Dog;" b. "The Plymouth Express;" c. "The Affair at the Victory Ball;" d. "The Market Basing Mystery;" e. "The Lemesurier Inheritance;" f. "The Cornish Mystery;" g. "The King of Clubs;" h. "The Submarine Plans;" i. "The Adventure of the Clapham Cook."

31. *Blood Will Tell.* London: Collins, 1952; New York: Dodd, Mead, 1952 [*Mrs. McGinty's Dead*]; New York: Pocket Books, 1953; London: Fontana Books, 1957; London: Pan Books, 1970.

32. *After the Funeral.* London: Collins, 1953; New York: Dodd, Mead, 1953 [*Funerals Are Fatal*]; New York: Black, 1953; New York: Pocket Books, 1954; London: Fontana Books, 1963 [*Murder at the Gallop*]; Leicester, Eng.: Ulverscroft, 1968 (large print).

[/G/ *Christie Classics.* New York: Dodd, Mead, 1954. (Includes: I:4; XI:4; I:28; I:29)]

33. *Hickory, Dickory, Dock.* London: Collins, 1955; New York: Dodd, Mead, 1955 [*Hickory, Dickory, Death*]; New York: Pocket Books, 1956; London: Fontana Books, 1958; London: Pan Books, 1967.

34. *Dead Man's Folly.* London: Collins, 1956; New York: Dodd, Mead, 1956; London: Book Club, 1957; New York: Pocket Books, 1957; London: Fontana Books, 1960; London: Pan Books, 1966; Leicester, Eng.: Ulverscroft, 1967 (large print).

[/H/ *Surprise Endings by Hercule Poirot.* New York: Dodd, Mead, 1956. (Includes: I:12; I:10; I:14)]

35. *Cat among the Pigeons.* London: Collins, 1959; New York: Dodd, Mead, 1960; New York: Pocket Books, 1961;

London: Fontana Books, 1962; Leicester, Eng.: Ulverscroft, 1964 (large print).

36. *The Adventure of the Christmas Pudding.* London: Collins, 1960; London: Fontana Books, 1963; London: Pan Books, 1969.

    a. "The Adventure of the Christmas Pudding" (**Poirot**) [identical with I:37:c]; b. "The Mystery of the Spanish Chest" (**Poirot**) [cf. "The Mystery of the Baghdad Chest": I:20:b]; c. "The Under Dog" (**Poirot**); d. "Four and Twenty Blackbirds" (**Poirot**); e. "The Dream" (**Poirot**); f. "Greenshaw's Folly" (**Marple**).

[/J/ *Murder Preferred.* New York: Dodd, Mead, 1960. (Includes: I:21; II:7; I:24)]

37. *Double Sin.* New York: Dodd, Mead, 1961; New York: Pocket Books, 1962; New York: Dell, 1964.

    a. "Double Sin" (**Poirot**); b. "Wasps' Nest" (**Poirot**); c. "The Theft of the Royal Ruby" (**Poirot**) [identical with I:36:a]; d. "The Dressmaker's Doll" (none); e. "Greenshaw's Folly" (**Marple**); f. "The Double Clue" (**Poirot**); g. "The Last Séance" (none); h. "Sanctuary" (**Marple**).

38. *13 for Luck.* New York: Dodd, Mead, 1961; New York: Dell, 1965; London: Collins, 1966.

    a. "The Veiled Lady" (**Poirot**); b. "The Nemean Lion" (**Poirot**); c. "The Girdle of Hippolyta" (**Poirot**); d. "The Market Basing Mystery" (**Poirot**); e. "Tape-Measure Murder" (**Marple**); f. "The Blue Geranium" (**Marple**); g. "The Four Suspects" (**Marple**); h. "The Face of Helen" (**Quin**); i. "The Bird with the Broken Wing" (**Quin**); j. "The Regatta Mystery" (**Pyne**); k. "Problem at Pollensa Bay" (**Pyne**); l. "The Unbreakable Alibi" (**Tommy and Tuppence**); m. "Accident" (none).

[/K/ *Make Mine Murder.* New York: Dodd, Mead, 1962; New York: Dell, 1963. (Includes: I:18; I:7; I:22)]

39. *The Clocks.* London: Collins, 1963; New York: Dodd, Mead, 1964; New York: Pocket Books, 1965; London: Fontana Books, 1967; Leicester, Eng.: Ulverscroft, 1969 (large print).

[/L/ *Murder International.* New York: Dodd, Mead, 1965. (Includes: XI:9; XI:5; I:23)]

40. *Surprise! Surprise!* New York: Dodd, Mead, 1965; New York: Dell, 1966.

    a. "Double Sin" (**Poirot**); b. "The Arcadian Deer" (**Poirot**); c. "The Adventure of Johnny Waverly" (**Poirot**); d. "Where There's a Will" (none) [British title: "Wireless": XI:1:f]; e. "Greenshaw's Folly" (**Marple**); f. "The Case of the Perfect Maid" (**Marple**); g. "At the Bells and Motley" (**Quin**); h. "The Case of the Distressed Lady" (**Pyne**); i. "The Third-

Floor Flat" (**Poirot**); j. "The Plymouth Express" (**Poirot**);
k. "The Mystery of the Spanish Shawl" (none); l. "The
Cornish Mystery" (**Poirot**); m. "The Witness for the
Prosecution" (none).

41. *The Third Girl.* London: Collins, 1966; New York: Dodd,
Mead, 1967; New York: Pocket Books, 1968; Leicester, Eng.:
Ulverscroft, 1968 (large print); London: Fontana Books, 1969.
[/M/ *Spies among Us.* New York: Dodd, Mead, 1968.
(Includes: XI:7; III:3; I:13)]

42. *Hallowe'en Party.* London: Collins, 1969; New York:
Dodd, Mead, 1969; New York: Pocket Books, 1970; London:
Fontana Books, 1972.
[/N/ *The Nursery Rhyme Murders.* New York: Dodd, Mead,
1970. (Includes: II:7; I:33; XI:7)]

43. *Elephants Can Remember.* London: Collins, 1972; New
York: Dodd, Mead, 1972; New York: Dell, 1973; Boston: Hall,
1973 (large print); London: Fontana, 1974.
[/O/ *Murder-Go-Round.* New York: Dodd, Mead, 1972.
(Includes: I:8; I:12; I:32)]
[/P/ *Poirot's Early Cases.* London: Collins, 1974; Boston:
Hall, 1975 (large print); London: Fontana, 1979. (Includes:
I:30:c; I:30:i; I:30:f; I:29:g; I:37:f; I:30:g; I:30:e; I:3:m; I:30:b;
I:3:n; I:30:h; I:29:f; I:37:a; I:30:d; I:37:b; I:3:l; I:20:i; I:20:c)]
[/Q/ *Murder on Board.* New York: Dodd, Mead, 1974.
(Includes: I:6; II:8; I:11)]

44. *Curtain.* New York: Dodd, Mead, 1975; London: Collins,
1975, New York: Pocket Books, 1976; Leicester, Eng.:
Ulverscroft, 1976 (large print); London: Fontana, 1977.

II. Jane Marple

1. *The Murder at the Vicarage.* New York: Dodd, Mead,
1930; London: Collins, 1930; New York: Grosset and Dunlap,
1932; London: Penguin Books, 1948; New York: Dell, 1955;
London: Fontana Books, 1961.

2. *The Thirteen Problems.* London: Collins, 1932; New
York: Dodd, Mead, 1933 (*The Tuesday Club Murders*); New
York: Grosset and Dunlap, 1933; New York: Dell, 1942;
London: Penguin Books, 1953; London: Pan Books, 1961;
London: Fontana Books, 1965; Leicester, Eng.: Ulverscroft,
1971 (large print).

(All **Marple**) a. "The Tuesday Night Club;" b. "The Idol
House of Astarte;" c. "Ingots of Gold;" d. "The Bloodstained
Pavement;" e. "Motive v. Opportunity;" f. "The Thumb
Mark of St. Peter;" g. "The Blue Geranium;" h. "The
Companion;" i. "The Four Suspects;" j. "A Christmas
Tragedy;" k. "The Herb of Death;" l. "The Affair at the

Bungalow;" m. "Death by Drowning."
[*The Regatta Mystery*. (For full list of publishers and short-story titles I:20). (Includes: I:20:f: "Miss Marple Tells a Story")]

3. *The Body in the Library*. London: Collins, 1942; New York: Dodd, Mead, 1942; New York: Collier, 1942; New York: Grosset and Dunlap, 1942; New York: Pocket Books, 1946; London: Penguin Books, 1953; London: Pan Books, 1959; London: Fontana Books, 1967; Leicester, Eng.: Ulverscroft, 1972 (large print).

4. *The Moving Finger*. New York: Dodd, Mead, 1942; New York: American Mercury, 1942; New York: Dell, 1942; London: Collins, 1943; London: Pan Books, 1948; New York: Avon Books, 1948; New York: American Book Co., 1948; London: Penguin Books, 1953; London: Fontana Books, 1961; Leicester, Eng.: Ulverscroft, 1970 (large print).

[*Three Blind Mice*. (For full list of publishers and short-story titles *v*. I:29). (Includes: I:29:b: "Strange Jest;" I:29:c: "Tape-Measure Murder;" I:29:d: "The Case of the Perfect Maid;" I:29:e: "The Case of the Caretaker")]

5. *A Murder Is Announced*. London: Collins, 1950; New York: Dodd, Mead, 1950; New York: Black, 1950; London: Fontana Books, 1953; London: Pan Books, 1958; Leicester, Eng.: Ulverscroft, 1965 (large print); New York: Pocket Books, 1967.

6. *Murder with Mirrors*. New York: Dodd, Mead, 1952; London: Collins, 1952 [*They Do It with Mirrors*]; New York: Pocket Books, 1954; London: Fontana Books, 1956; Leicester, Eng.: Ulverscroft, 1966 (large print); London: Pan Books, 1971.

7. *A Pocket Full of Rye*. London: Collins, 1953; New York: Dodd, Mead, 1954; London: Fontana Books, 1958; Leicester, Eng.: Ulverscroft, 1964 (large print); New York: Pocket Books, 1967.

8. *The 4:50 from Paddington*. London: Collins, 1957; New York: Dodd, Mead, 1957 [*What Mrs. McGillicuddy Saw*]; London: Fontana Books, 1960; New York: Pocket Books, 1961 [*Murder, She Said*]; Leicester, Eng.: Ulverscroft, 1965 (large print); London: Pan Books, 1974.

[*The Adventure of the Christmas Pudding*. (For full list of publishers and short-story titles *v*. I:36). (Includes: I:36:e: "Greenshaw's Folly")]

[/J/ *Murder Preferred*. New York: Dodd, Mead, 1960. (Includes: I:21; II:7; I:24)]

[*Double Sin*. (For full list of publishers and short-story titles *v*. I:37). (Includes: I:37:e: "Greenshaw's Folly;" I:37:h: "Sanctuary")]

[*Thirteen for Luck*. (For full list of publishers and short-story titles *v.* I:38). (Includes: I:38:e: "Tape-Measure Murder;" I:38:f: "The Blue Geranium;" I:38:g: "The Four Suspects")]

9. *The Mirror Crack'd from Side to Side.* London: Collins, 1962; New York: Dodd, Mead, 1963 [*The Mirror Crack'd*]; London: Fontana Books, 1965; Leicester, Eng.: Ulverscroft, 1966 (large print); New York: Pocket Books, 1970.

10. *A Caribbean Mystery.* London: Collins, 1964; New York: Dodd, Mead, 1965; London: Fontana Books, 1966; Leicester, Eng.: Ulverscroft, 1966 (large print); New York: Pocket Books, 1970.

11. *At Bertram's Hotel.* London: Collins, 1965; New York: Dodd, Mead, 1966; Roslyn, N.Y.: Black, 1966; New York: Pocket Books, 1967; London: Fontana Books, 1968; Leicester, Eng.: Ulverscroft, 1968 (large print).

[*Surprise! Surprise!* (For full list of publishers and short-story titles *v.* I:40). (Includes: I:40:e: "Greenshaw's Folly;" I:40:f: "The Case of the Perfect Maid")]

12. *13 Clues for Miss Marple.* New York: Dodd, Mead, 1967; New York: Dell, 1967.

(All **Marple**) a. "Tape-Measure Murder;" b. "Strange Jest;" c. "Sanctuary;" d. "Greenshaw's Folly;" e. "The Case of the Perfect Maid;" f. "The Case of the Caretaker;" g. "The Blue Geranium;" h. "The Companion;" i. "The Four Suspects;" j. "Motive *v.* Opportunity;" k. "The Thumb Mark of St. Peter;" l. "The Bloodstained Pavement;" m. "The Herb of Death."

[/R/ *Murder in Our Midst*. New York: Dodd, Mead, 1967. (Includes: II:3; II:1; II:4).

[/N/ *The Nursery Rhyme Murders*. New York: Dodd, Mead, 1970. (Includes: II:7; I:33; XI:7)]

13. *Nemesis.* London: Collins, 1971; New York: Dodd, Mead, 1971; New York: Pocket Books, 1973; London: Fontana, 1975; Leicester, Eng.: Ulverscroft, 1976 (large print).

14. *Sleeping Murder.* London: Collins, 1976; New York: Dodd, Mead, 1976; New York: Bantam Books, 1977; London: Fontana, 1978.

III. Tommy and Tuppence Beresford

1. *The Secret Adversary.* London: Lane, 1922; New York: Dodd, Mead, 1922; New York: Grosset and Dunlap, 1931; London: Pan Books, 1955; New York: Bantam Books, 1967.

2. *Partners in Crime.* London: Collins, 1929; New York: Dodd, Mead, 1929; New York: Grosset and Dunlap, 1929; New York: L.E. Spivak, 1929 (abridged); London: Fontana Books, 1958; London: Pan Books, 1962; New York: Dell, 1963.

(All **Tommy and Tuppence**) a. "A Fairy in the Flat;" b. "A Pot of Tea;" c. "The Affair of the Pink Pearl" (2 parts); d.

"The Adventure of the Sinister Stranger" (2 parts); e. "Finessing the King;" f. "The Gentleman Dressed in Newspaper;" g. "The Case of the Missing Lady;" h. "Blindman's Buff;" i. "The Man in the Mist" (2 parts); j. "The Crackler" (2 parts); k. "The Sunningdale Mystery" (2 parts); l. "The House of Lurking Death" (2 parts); m. "The Unbreakable Alibi;" n. "The Clergyman's Daughter;" o. "The Red House;" p. "The Ambassador's Boots;" q. "The Man Who Was No. 16."

3. *N or M?* London: Collins, 1941; New York: Dodd, Mead, 1941; New York: Dell, 1953; London: Pan Books, 1959; London: Fontana Books, 1962.

[*Thirteen for Luck.* (For full list of publishers and short-story titles *v.* I:38). (Includes: I:38:l: "The Unbreakable Alibi")]

[/E/ *Triple Threat; Exploits of Three Famous Detectives: Hercule Poirot, Harley Quin, and Tuppence.* New York: Dodd, Mead, 1943. (Includes: I:3; V:l; III:2)]

4. *By the Pricking of My Thumbs.* London: Collins, 1968; New York: Dodd, Mead, 1968; New York: Pocket Books, 1969; London: Fontana Books, 1971.

[/M/ *Spies among Us.* New York: Dodd, Mead, 1968. (Includes: XI:7; III:3; I:13)]

5. *Postern of Fate.* London: Crime Club, 1973; New York: Dodd, Mead, 1973; New York: Bantam Books, 1974; Boston: Hall, 1974 (large print); London: Fontana, 1976.

IV. Parker Pyne

1. *Parker Pyne Investigates.* London: Collins, 1934; New York: Dodd, Mead, 1934 [*Mr. Parker Pyne, Detective*]; London: Penguin Books, 1953; New York: Dell, 1953; London: Fontana Books, 1962; London: Pan Books, 1968.

(All **Pyne**) a. "The Case of the Middle-Aged Wife;" b. "The Case of the Discontented Soldier;" c. "The Case of the Distressed Lady;" d. "The Case of the Discontented Husband;" e. "The Case of the City Clerk;" f. "The Case of the Rich Woman;" g. "Have You Got Everything You Want?;" h. "The Gate of Baghdad;" i. "The House at Shiraz;" j. "The Pearl of Price;" k. "Death on the Nile" [the novel with an identical title is unrelated to this short story]; l. "The Oracle at Delphi."

[*The Regatta Mystery.* (For full list of publishers and short-story titles *v.* I:20). (Includes: I:20:a: "The Regatta Mystery;" I:20:d: "Problem at Pollensa Bay")]

[*Surprise! Surprise!* (For full list of publishers and short-story titles *v.* I:40). (Includes: I:40:h: "The Case of the Distressed Lady")]

V. Harley Quin

 1. *The Mysterious Mr. Quin.* London: Collins, 1930; New York: Dodd, Mead, 1930; New York: L.E. Spivak, 1930 (abridged); London: Penguin Books, 1953; New York: Dell, 1955; London: Fontana Books, 1964; London: Pan Books, 1973; Leicester, Eng.: Ulverscroft, 1977 (large print). (All **Quin**) a. "The Coming of Mr. Quin;" b. "The Shadow on the Glass;" c. "At the Bells and Motley;" d. "The Sign in the Sky;" e. "The Soul of the Croupier;" f. "The World's End;" g. "The Voice in the Dark;" h. "The Face of Helen;" i. "The Dead Harlequin;" j. "The Bird with the Broken Wing;" k. "The Man from the Sea;" l. "Harlequin's Lane."

 [/E/ *Triple Threat; Exploits of Three Famous Detectives: Hercule Poirot, Harley Quin, and Tuppence.* New York: Dodd, Mead, 1943. (Includes: I:3; V:l; III:2)]

 [*Thirteen for Luck.* (For full list of publishers and short-story titles *v.* I:38). (Includes: I:38h: "The Face of Helen;" I:38:i: "The Bird with the Broken Wing")]

 [*Surprise! Surprise!* (For full list of publishers and short-story titles *v.* I:40). (Includes: I:40:g: "At the Bells and Motley")]

VI. Superintendent Battle

 1. *The Secret of Chimneys.* London: Lane, 1925; New York: Dodd, Mead, 1925; New York: Grosset and Dunlap, 1927; New York: Dell, 1945; London: Penguin Books, 1948; London: Fontana Books, 1954; London: Pan Books, 1956.

 2. *The Seven Dials Mystery.* London: Collins, 1929; New York: Dodd, Mead, 1929; New York: Bantam Books, 1929; New York: Grosset and Dunlap, 1930; New York: Books, Inc., 1944; London: Fontana Books, 1954; London: Pan Books, 1962.

 [/B/ *The Agatha Christie Omnibus of Crime.* London: Collins, 1932. (Includes: X:1; VI:2; I:6; I:4)]

 3. *Murder Is Easy.* London: Collins, 1939; New York: Dodd, Mead, 1939 [*Easy to Kill*]; New York: Grosset and Dunlap, 1939; New York: Pocket Books, 1945; London: Pan Books, 1951; London: Penguin Books, 1957; London: Fontana Books, 1960; Leicester, Eng.: Ulverscroft, 1966 (large print).

 4. *Towards Zero.* London: Collins, 1944; New York: Dodd, Mead, 1944; New York: Pocket Books, 1947; London: Pan Books, 1948; London: Fontana Books, 1959; Leicester, Eng.: Ulverscroft, 1972 (large print).

VII. Colonel John Race

 1. *The Man in the Brown Suit.* London: Lane, 1924; New York: Dodd, Mead, 1924; New York: Grosset and Dunlap, 1924; New York: Dell, 1952; London: Pan Books, 1953.

2. *Sparkling Cyanide.* London: Collins, 1945; New York: Dodd, Mead, 1945 [*Remembered Death*]; New York: Grosset and Dunlap, 1946; New York: Pocket Books, 1947; London: Pan Books, 1955; London: Fontana Books, 1960.

VIII. Mark Easterbrook
1. *The Pale Horse.* London: Collins, 1961; New York: Dodd, Mead, 1962; New York: Pocket Books, 1963; London: Fontana Books, 1964; Leicester, Eng.: Ulverscroft, 1965 (large print).

IX. Arthur Calgary
1. *Ordeal by Innocence.* London: Collins, 1958; New York: Dodd, Mead, 1959; New York: Pocket Books, 1960; London: Fontana Books, 1961; Leicester, Eng.: Ulverscroft, 1969 (large print).

X. Inspector Narracott
1. *The Sittaford Mystery.* London: Collins, 1931; New York: Dodd, Mead, 1931 [*Murder at Hazelmoor*]; London: Penguin Books, 1948; New York: Dell, 1952; London: Fontana Books, 1961; London: Pan books, 1965; Leicester, Eng.: Ulverscroft, 1973 (large print).

XI. Stories without a Central Detective
1. *The Hound of Death.* London: Oldham's Press, 1933; London: Collins, 1936; London: Pan Books, 1960; London: Fontana Books, 1964; Leicester, Eng.: Ulverscroft, 1968 (large print).
   a. "The Hound of Death;" b. "The Red Signal;" c. "The Fourth Man;" d. "The Gipsy;" e. "The Lamp;" f. "Wireless" [American title: "Where There's a Will"]; g. "The Witness for the Prosecution;" h. "The Mystery of the Blue Jar;" i. "The Strange Case of Sir Arthur Carmichael;" j. "The Call of Wings;" k. "The Last Seance;" l. "S.O.S."
2. *Why Didn't They Ask Evans?* London: Collins, 1934; New York: Dodd, Mead, 1935 [*The Boomerang Clue*]; New York: Dell, 1943; London: Fontana Books, 1956; London: Pan Books, 1968; Leicester, Eng.: Ulverscroft, 1974 (large print).
3. *The Listerdale Mystery.* London: Collins, 1934; London: Fontana Books, 1961; London: Pan Books, 1970.
   a. "The Listerdale Mystery;" b. "Philomel Cottage;" c. "The Girl in the Train;" d. "Sing a Song of Sixpence;" e. "The Manhood of Edward Robinson;" f. "Accident;" g. "Jane in Search of a Job;" h. "A Fruitful Sunday;" i. "Mr. Eastwood's Adventure;" j. "The Golden Ball;" k. "The Rajah's Emerald;" l. "Swan Song."
4. *Ten Little Niggers.* London: Collins, 1939; New York:

Dodd, Mead, 1940 [*And Then There Were None*]; New York: Grosset and Dunlap, 1940; New York: Pocket Books, 1944 [*Ten Little Indians*]; London: Pan Books, 1947; London: Fontana Books, 1963; New York: Washington Square Press, 1964.

5. *Death Comes as the End.* New York: Dodd, Mead, 1944; London: Collins, 1945; London: Penguin Books, 1953; London: Fontana Books, 1960; London: Pan Books, 1963; New York: Pocket Books, 1968; Leicester, Eng.: Ulverscroft, 1970 (large print).

6. *Crooked House.* London: Collins, 1949; New York: Dodd, Mead, 1949; New York: Pocket Books, 1950; London: Penguin Books, 1953; London: Fontana Books, 1959; Leicester, Eng.: Ulverscroft, 1968 (large print).

7. *They Came to Baghdad.* London: Collins, 1951; New York: Dodd, Mead, 1951; London: Fontana Books, 1957; New York: Dell, 1965; Leicester, Eng.: Ulverscroft, 1965 (large print); London: Pan Books, 1974.

8. *Destination Unknown.* London: Collins, 1954; New York: Dodd, Mead, 1955 [*So Many Steps to Death*]; New York: Pocket Books, 1956; London: Fontana Books, 1958; Leicester, Eng.: Ulverscroft, 1971 (large print).

9. *Endless Night.* London: Collins, 1967; New York: Dodd, Mead, 1968; New York: Pocket Books, 1969; London: Fontana Books, 1970; Leicester, Eng.: Ulverscroft, 1972 (large print).

10. Passenger to Frankfurt. London: Collins, 1970; New York Dodd, Mead, 1970; New York: Pocket Books, 1973; London: Fontana Books, 1973.

11. *The Golden Ball.* New York: Dodd, Mead, 1971; New York: Dell, 1972.
a. "The Listerdale Mystery;" b. "The Girl in the Train;" c. "The Manhood of Edward Robinson;" d. "Jane in Search of a Job;" e. "A Fruitful Sunday;" f. "The Golden Ball;" g. "The Rajah's Emerald;" h. "Swan Song;" i. "The Hound of Death;" j. "The Gipsy;" k. "The Lamp;" l. "The Strange Case of Sir Andrew Carmichael" [note difference in first name from that in XI:1:i]; m. "The Call of Wings;" n. "Magnolia Blossom;" o. "Next to a Dog."

XII. Miscellaneous
A. Novels under Mary Westmacott pseudonym
1. *Giant's Bread.* London: Collins, 1930; New York: Doubleday, Doran, 1930; New York: Dell, 1964; New York: Arbor House, 1973.

2. *Unfinished Portrait.* Garden City, N.Y.: Doubleday, Doran, 1934; New York: Dell, 1964; New York: Arbor House,

1972.

3. *Absent in the Spring.* London: Collins, 1944; New York: Rinehart, 1948; New York: Dell, 1963; New York: Arbor House, 1971.

4. *The Rose and the Yew Tree.* London: Heinemann, 1947; New York: Rinehart, 1948; New York: Dell, 1964; New York: Arbor House, 1971.

5. *A Daughter's a Daughter.* London: Heinemann, 1952; New York: Dell, 1963; New York: Arbor House, 1972.

6. *The Burden.* London: Heinemann, 1956; New York: Dell, 1963; New York: Arbor House, 1973.

B. Poetry

    1. *The Road of Dreams.* London: Bles, 1925.

    2. *Star over Bethlehem and Other Stories.* London: Collins, 1965; New York: Dodd, Mead, 1965. [Author's name given as Agatha Christie Mallowan.]

    3. *And Then There Were None.* Philadelphia: Fronheiser, 1970.

    4. *Poems.* London: Collins, 1973; New York: Dodd, Mead, 1973. [Incorporates, as "Volume One," *The Road of Dreams.*]

C. Archeology

    1. *Come, Tell Me How You Live.* London: Collins, 1946; New York: Dodd, Mead, 1946.

D. Plays

    1. *Alibi.* London: French, 1929. [Adapted from novel *The Murder of Roger Ackroyd;* dramatized by Michael Morton; produced London, 1928.]

    2. *Black Coffee.* London: Ashley, 1934. [Original play; produced London, 1930.]

    3. *Love from a Stranger.* London: Collins, 1936; London: French, 1937. [Adapted from short story "Philomel Cottage"; dramatized by author and Frank Vosper; produced London, 1936.]

    4. *Ten Little Niggers.* London: French, 1945; New York: French, 1946 [*Ten Little Indians*]. [Adapted from novel of same title; dramatized by author; produced Wimbledon and London, 1943; New York, 1944.]

    5. *Peril at End House.* London: French, 1945. [Adapted from novel of same title; dramatized by Arnold Ridley; produced London, 1940.]

    6. *Appointment with Death.* London: French, 1945. [Adapted from novel of same title; dramatized by author; produced Glasgow and London, 1945.]

    7. *Murder on the Nile.* London: French, 1948. [Adapted from

novel *Death on the Nile*; dramatized by author; produced
Wimbledon, 1945; London and New York, 1946 (in New York
with title *Hidden Horizon*).]
8. *Murder at the Vicarage.* London: French, 1950. [Adapted
from novel of same title; dramatized by Moie Charles and
Barbara Toy; produced London, 1949.]
9. *The Hollow.* London: French, 1952. [Adapted from novel
of same title; dramatized by author; produced Cambridge and
London, 1951; Princeton, N.J., 1952.]
10. *The Mousetrap.* London: French, 1954. [Adapted from
short story "Three Blind Mice"; dramatized by author;
written originally as a radio play, broadcast by BBC, 1952;
revised version produced Nottingham and London, 1952;
New York, 1960. (*Note:* This play established records never
before equaled on the legitimate stage. After a seven-week
tour opening in Nottingham on October 6, 1952, it transferred
to the Ambassador Theatre, London, on November 25, 1952,
and to St. Martin's Theatre, London, on March 23, 1974,
where it is still playing. On December 17, 1976, it reached its
10,000th London performance. Its cast has included 140
actors and actresses. It has been presented in forty-one other
countries.

With Prime Minister James Callaghan as the most noted
guest, the twenty-fifth anniversary of the London run of *The
Mousetrap* was celebrated by an elaborate lunch at the Savoy
Hotel on November 25, 1977. Producer Saunders was that
night presenting the 10,391st London performance of the
fabulous play. The Prime Minister toasted the occasion in
orange juice. Many of the more than 1,000 guests would see
the play that night, some for the first time, others in nostalgic
recollection of earlier visits. It was said that by then the play
had been seen by more than four million people.

"If the takings at the London box office," said Sir
Richard Attenborough who had played Detective Sergeant
Trotter in the original cast, "were all paid in one pound notes
and laid end to end, they would stretch from London to
Geneva." The hotel orchestra struck an appropriate note
when it played "It Was Just One of Those Things").]
11. *Witness for the Prosecution.* London: French, 1954; New
York: French, 1957. [Adapted from short story of same title;
dramatized by author; produced Nottingham and London,
1953; New York, 1954.]
12. *The Spider's Web.* London: French, 1956. [Original play;
produced Nottingham and London, 1954.]
13. *Towards Zero.* London: French, 1957; New York:
Dramatists Play Service, 1957. [Adapted from novel of same
title; dramatized by author; produced Nottingham and

London, 1956.]
14.   *Verdict.* London: French, 1958.[Original play; produced
Wolverhampton and London, 1958.]
15.   *The Unexpected Guest.* London: French, 1958.[Original
play; produced London, 1959.]
16.   *Go Back for Murder.* London: French, 1960. [Adapted
from novel *Five Little Pigs;* dramatized by author; produced
Edinburgh and London, 1960.]
17.   *Rule of Three.* London: French, 1963. [Three original
one-act plays: Afternoon at the Seaside; The Patient; The
Rats; produced at Aberdeen and London, 1962.]
18.   *Fiddlers Three.* London: French, 1972. [Original play;
produced Southsea, 1971.]
19.   *Akhnaton.* London: Collins, 1973; New York: Dodd,
Mead, 1973. [Original play.]
20.   *Murder Is Announced.* [Adapted from novel of same
title; dramatized by Leslie Darbon; produced London, 1977.]

E. Motion Pictures
1.   *The Passing of Mr. Quin* [based on the Mr. Quin stories].
England, 1928; Strand. Stewart Rome.
2.   *Black Coffee* [based on play of same title]. England, 1931;
Twickenham Films. Austin Trevor as Poirot; Richard Cooper.
3.   *Alibi* [based on novel *The Murder of Roger Ackroyd*].
England, 1931; Twickenham Films. Austin Trevor as Poirot.
4.   *Lord Edgware Dies* [based on novel of same title].
England, 1934; Real Art. Austin Trevor as Poirot.
5.   *Love from a Stranger* [based on short story "Philomel
Cottage"]. England, 1937; Eagle Lion; United Artists. Basil
Rathbone, Ann Harding. (Same). England, 1947; Eagle Lion.
John Hodiak, Sylvia Sidney.
6.   *Ten Little Niggers* (released in U.S.A. with title *And Then
There Were None*) [based on play of same title]. England,
1945; Twentieth Century-Fox. Barry Fitzgerald as the Judge;
Walter Huston, Louis Hayward, Roland Young, June Duprez.
(Same; with title *Ten Little Indians*). U.S.A., 1965; Seven
Arts; England, 1965; ABP [Associated British Productions].
Wilford Hyde as the Judge; Shirley Eaton, Stanley Holloway.
(Same; with title *And Then There Were None*). England, 1974;
Avco Embassy. Richard Attenborough, Herbert Lom, Elke
Sommer.
7.   *Witness for the Prosecution* [based on play of same title].
England, 1957; Edward Small; United Artists. Charles
Laughton as the advocate; Tyrone Power, Marlene Dietrich,
Elsa Lanchester.
8.   *The Spider's Web* [based on play of same title]. U.S.A.,
1960; United Artists. Glynis Johns, John Justin.

9. *Murder, She Said* [based on novel *The 4:50 from Paddington*]. England, 1961; MGM. Margaret Rutherford as Miss Marple; Arthur Kennedy, Muriel Pavlov, James Robertson.
10. *Murder Most Foul* [based on novel *Blood Will Tell*]. England, 1963; MGM. Margaret Rutherford as Miss Marple substituted for Poirot.
11. *Murder at the Gallop* [based on novel *After the Funeral*]. England, 1963; MGM. Margaret Rutherford as Miss Marple substituted for Poirot.
12. *Murder Ahoy* [based on Miss Marple stories; not written by Mrs. Christie]. England, 1964; MGM. Margaret Rutherford as Miss Marple.
13. *The Alphabet Murders* [based on novel *The A.B.C. Murders*]. U.S.A., 1966; MGM. Tony Randall as Poirot; Anita Ekberg, Robert Morley.
14. *Murder on the Orient Express* [based on novel of same title]. U.S.A., 1974; Paramount. Albert Finney as Poirot; Lauren Bacall, Ingrid Bergman, Sean Connery, John Gielgud, Vanessa Redgrave.
15. *Death on the Nile* [based on novel of same title]. U.S.A., 1978; Paramount. Peter Ustinov as Poirot; Bette Davis, Angela Lansbury, David Niven, Olivia Hussey.

Alphabetical List of Christie Detective and Mystery Story Titles

All detective and mystery book and short-story titles (but not other Christie writings) are here entered in one list, with coded identification of items conforming to that used in the Master Bibliography. Entries in italics indicate books, those in roman are titles of short stories. Citations are to the imprint of first publication, whether British or American. Citations to short stories are to the first entry in the Master Bibliography; for other locations of the same stories consult the **Short Story FINDER.**

Guide to *detectives:* I: **Poirot;** II: **Marple;** III: **Tommy-Tuppence;** IV: **Pyne;** V: **Quin;** VI: **Battle;** VII: **Race;** VIII: **Easterbrook;** IX: **Calgary;** X: **Narracott;** XI: **none.**

The A.B.C. Murders. I:12
"Accident." I:28:h
"The Adventure of Johnny Waverly." I:29:g
"The Adventure of the Cheap Flat." I:3:c
The Adventure of the Christmas Pudding. I:36
"The Adventure of the Christmas Pudding." I:36:a
"The Adventure of the Clapham Cook." I:30:i
"The Adventure of the Egyptian Tomb." I:3:f
"The Adventure of the Italian Nobleman." I:3:j
"The Adventure of the Sinister Stranger." III:2:d
"The Adventure of The Western Star." I:3:a
"The Affair at the Bungalow." II:2:l
"The Affair at the Victory Ball." I:30:c
"The Affair of the Pink Pearl." III:2:c
After the Funeral. I:32
"The Ambassador's Boots." III:2:p
And Then There Were None; see *Ten Little Niggers.* XI:4
"The Apples of the Hesperides." I:26:l
Appointment with Death. I:18
"The Arcadian Deer." I:26:d
At Bertram's Hotel. II:11
"At the Bells and Motley." I:40:g

Mr. Parker Pyne, Detective; see *Parker Pyne Investigates.* IV:1
Mrs. McGinty's Dead; see *Blood Will Tell.* I:31
Murder after Hours; see *The Hollow.* I:25
Murder at Hazelmoor; see *The Sittaford Mystery.* X:1
Murder at Littlegreen House; see *Dumb Witness.* I:15
Murder at the Gallop; see *After the Funeral.* I:32
Murder at the Vicarage. II:1
Murder for Christmas; see *Hercule Poirot's Christmas.* I:19
Murder in Mesopotamia. I:13
Murder in Retrospect. I:24
Murder in the Calais Coach; see *Murder on the Orient Express.* I:9
Murder in the Mews. I:17
"Murder in the Mews." I:17:a
Murder in Three Acts. I:10
A Murder Is Announced. II:5
Murder Is Easy. VI:3
The Murder of Roger Ackroyd. I:4
Murder on the Links. I:2
Murder on the Orient Express. I:9
Murder, She Said; see *The 4:50 from Paddington.* II:8
Murder with Mirrors. II:6
The Mysterious Affair at Styles. I:1
The Mysterious Mr. Quin. V:1
Mystery at Littlegreen House; see *Dumb Witness.* I:15
"The Mystery of Hunter's Lodge." I:3:d
"The Mystery of the Baghdad Chest." I:20:b
"The Mystery of the Blue Jar." I:28:f
The Mystery of the Blue Train. I:6
"The Mystery of the Spanish Chest." I:36:b
"The Mystery of the Spanish Shawl." I:40:k

N or M? III:3
"The Nemean Lion." I:26:b
Nemesis. II:13
"Next to a Dog." XI:11:o

One, Two, Buckle My Shoe. I:21
"The Oracle at Delphi." IV:1:l
Ordeal by Innocence. IX:1
An Overdose of Death; see *One, Two, Buckle My Shoe.* I:21

The Pale Horse. VIII:1
Parker Pyne Investigates. IV:1
Partners in Crime. III:2
Passenger to Frankfurt. XI:10
The Patriotic Murders; see *One, Two, Buckle My Shoe.* I:21
"The Pearl of Price." IV:1:j

The Hound of Death uses the name Arthur; *The Golden Ball,* Andrew.

Alternate Christie Book Titles

After the Funeral = *Funerals Are Fatal* = *Murder at the Gallop*

And Then There Were None = *Ten Little Indians* = *Ten Little Niggers*

Blood Will Tell = *Mrs. McGinty's Dead*

The Boomerang Clue = *Why Didn't They Ask Evans?*

Come and Be Hanged = *Towards Zero*

Crime Reader = *Triple Threat: Exploits of Three Famous Detectives; Hercule Poirot, Harley Quin, and Tuppence.*

Dead Man's Mirror = *Murder in the Mews*

Death in the Air = *Death in the Clouds*

Death in the Clouds = *Death in the Air*

Destination Unknown = *So Many Steps to Death*

Dumb Witness = *Murder at Littlegreen House* = *Mystery at Littlegreen House* = *Poirot Loses a Client*

Easy to Kill = *Murder Is Easy*

Five Little Pigs = *Murder in Retrospect*

The 4:50 from Paddington = *Murder, She Said* = *What Mrs. McGillicuddy Saw*

Funerals Are Fatal = *After the Funeral* = *Murder at the Gallop*

Hercule Poirot, Master Detective = *Three Christie Crimes*

Hercule Poirot's Christmas = *A Holiday for Murder* = *Murder for Christmas*

Hickory, Dickory, Death = *Hickory, Dickory, Dock*

Hickory, Dickory, Dock = *Hickory, Dickory, Death*

A Holiday for Murder = *Hercule Poirot's Christmas* = *Murder for Christmas*

The Hollow = *Murder after Hours*

Lord Edgeware Dies = *13 at Dinner*

The Mirror Crack'd = *The Mirror Crack'd from Side to Side*

The Mirror Crack'd from Side to Side = *The Mirror Crack'd*

The Mousetrap = *Three Blind Mice*

Mr. Parker Pyne, Detective = *Parker Pyne Investigates*

Mrs. McGinty's Dead = *Blood Will Tell*

Murder after Hours = *The Hollow*

The Murder at Hazelmoor = *The Sittaford Mystery*

Murder at Littlegreen House = *Dumb Witness* = *Mystery at Littlegreen House* = *Poirot Loses a Client*

Murder at the Gallop = *After the Funeral* = *Funerals Are Fatal*

Murder for Christmas = *Hercule Poirot's Christmas* = *A Holiday for Murder*

Murder in Retrospect = Five Little Pigs
Murder in the Calais Coach = Murder on the Orient Express
Murder in the Mews = Dead Man's Mirror
Murder in Three Acts = A Three-Act Tragedy
Murder Is Easy = Easy to Kill
Murder on the Orient Express = Murder in the Calais Coach
Murder, She Said = The 4:50 from Paddington = What Mrs.
*   McGillicuddy Saw*
Murder with Mirrors = They Do It with Mirrors
The Mysterious Mr. Quin = The Passing of Mr. Quin
Mystery at Littlegreen House = Dumb Witness = Murder at
*   Littlegreen House = Poirot Loses a Client*
N or M = The Secret Adventure
One, Two, Buckle My Shoe = An Overdose of Death = The Patriotic
*   Murders*
An Overdose of Death = One, Two, Buckle My Shoe = The Patriotic
*   Murders*
Parker Pyne Investigates = Mr. Parker Pyne, Detective
The Passing of Mr. Quin = The Mysterious Mr. Quin
The Patriotic Murders = One, Two, Buckle My Shoe = An Overdose
*   of Death*
Poirot and the Regatta Mystery = The Regatta Mystery
Poirot Loses a Client = Dumb Witness = Murder at Littlegreen
*   House = Mystery at Littlegreen House*
The Regatta Mystery = Poirot and the Regatta Mystery
Remembered Death = Sparkling Cyanide
The Secret Adventure = N or M?
The Sittaford Mystery = The Murder at Hazelmoor
So Many Steps to Death = Destination Unknown
Sparkling Cyanide = Remembered Death
Taken at the Flood = There Is a Tide
Ten Little Indians = And Then There Were None = Ten Little
*   Niggers*
Ten Little Niggers = And Then There Were None = Ten Little
*   Indians*
There Is a Tide = Taken at the Flood
They Do It with Mirrors = Murder with Mirrors
13 at Dinner = Lord Edgeware Dies
The Thirteen Problems = The Tuesday Club Murders
A Three-Act Tragedy = Murder in Three Acts
Three Blind Mice = The Mousetrap
Three Christie Crimes = Hercule Poirot, Master Detective
Towards Zero = Come and Be Hanged
Triple Threat: Exploits of Three Famous Detectives; Hercule
*   Poirot, Harley Quin, and Tuppence = Crime Reader*
The Tuesday Club Murders = The Thirteen Problems
What Mrs. McGillicuddy Saw = The 4:50 from Paddington =

Murder, She Said
Why Didn't they Ask Evans? = The Boomerang Clue

The Short-Story FINDER
for Christie Collections

In addition to her many novels, Dame Agatha published approximately 150 short stories. These have been issued in nineteen volumes, listed in the Finder below (as in the master by-Christie Bibliography) by title of first publication. In numerous instances the same story is included—in two cases under differing titles—in more than one volume; the record appears to be in the case of one story printed in four separate volumes.

In the Finder below, the *collections* of short stories are given at the top, listed chronologically from left to right in order of first publication, with the identifying code number as used in the master bibliography following each. Thus, the first collection of Christie short stories was published in 1924 as *Poirot Investigates* and is coded as I:3, indicating that it was the third volume published (novels and short-story collections) in the group dealing with Hercule Poirot.

In many cases, both of book titles and story titles, some condensation has been used, always intelligibly, it is hoped, in order to perform a Procrustean feat of fitting a relatively long title into a limited space.

Story titles are listed alphabetically at the left of the successive pages. Titles employed are those used in the book of first-dated publication, whether British or American. In parentheses following each title is given an initial(s) indicating the "central detective," if any, involved in the particular story. These are as follows: (P) = Poirot; (M) = Marple; (TT) = Tommy and Tuppence; (PP) = Parker Pyne; (Q) = Quin; (B) = Battle; (R) = Race; (E) = Easterbrook; (C) = Calgary; (N) = Narracott; and (n) indicates that the story so designated has no central detective. Not all of the above initials will be found in the table indicating distribution of stories in collections, inasmuch as a few detectives appear only in novels and not in short stories, but the scheme of identification has been kept as most nearly paralleling that used in the master bibliography.

	1924: Poirot Investigates, I:3	1929: Partners in Crime, III:2	1930: Mysterious Mr. Quin, V:1	1932: Thirteen Problems, II:2	1933: Hound of Death, XI:1	1934: Listerdale Mystery, XI:3	1934: Parker Pyne Investigates, IV:1	1937: Murder in the Mews, I:17	1939: Regatta Mystery, I:20	1947: Labours of Hercules, I:26	1948: Witness for Prosecution, I:28	1950: Three Blind Mice, I:29	1951: The Under Dog, I:30	1960: Adventures of Xmas Pudding, I:36	1961: Double Sin, I:37	1961: Thirteen for Luck, I:38	1965: Surprise! Surprise! I:40	1966: 13 Clues for Miss Marple, II:12	1971: The Golden Ball, XI:12
(n)											x					x			
e of Johnny Waverly (P)												x					x		
e of the Cheap Flat (P)	x																		
e of the Christmas Pudding (P)														x					
e of the Clapham Cook (P)													x						
e of the Egyptian Tomb (P)	x																		
e of the Italian Nobleman (P)	x																		
e of the Sinister Stranger (TT)		x																	
e of the "Western Star" (P)	x																		
t the Bungalow (M)				x															
t the Victory Ball (P)													x						
f the Pink Pearl (TT)		x																	
or's Boots (TT)		x																	
f the Hesperides (P)										x									
Deer (P)										x							x		
ells and Motley (Q)			x														x		
tables (P)										x									
h the Broken Wing (Q)			x												x				
's Buff (TT)		x																	
ined Pavement (M)				x														x	
anium (M)				x												x		x	
wings (n)					x														x
of Cerberus (P)										x									
the Caretaker (M)												x						x	
the City Clerk (PP)							x												
the Discontented Husband (PP)							x												
the Discontented Soldier (PP)							x												
the Distressed Lady (PP)							x										x		
the Middle-Aged Wife (PP)							x												
the Missing Lady (TT)		x																	

	1924: Poirot Investigates, I:3	1929: Partners in Crime, III:2	1930: Mysterious Mr. Quin, V:1	1932: Thirteen Problems, II:2	1933: Hound of Death, XI:1	1934: Listerdale Mystery, XI:3	1934: Parker Pyne Investigates, IV:1	1937: Murder in the Mews, I:17	1939: Regatta Mystery, I:20	1947: Labours of Hercules, I:26	1948: Witness for Prosecution, I:28	1950: Three Blind Mice, I:29	1951: The Under Dog, I:30	1960: Adventures of Xmas Pudding, I:36	1961: Double Sin, I:37	1961: Thirteen for Luck, I:38
Case of the Missing Will (P)	x															
Case of the Perfect Maid (M)												x				
Case of the Rich Woman (PP)							x									
Chocolate Box (P)	x															
Christmas Tragedy (M)				x												
Clergyman's Daughter (TT)		x														
Coming of Mr. Quin (Q)			x													
Companion (n)				x												
Cornish Mystery (P)													x			
Crackler (TT)		x														
Cretan Bull (P)										x						
Dead Harlequin (Q)			x													
Dead Man's Mirror (P)								x								
Death by Drowning (M)				x												
Death on the Nile (PP)							x									
Disappearance of Mr. Davenheim (P)	x															
Double Clue (P)															x	
Double Sin (P)															x	
Dream (P)									x					x		
Dressmaker's Doll (n)															x	
Erymanthian Boar (P)										x						
Face of Helen (Q)			x													x
Fairy in the Flat (TT)		x														
Finessing the King (TT)		x														
Flock of Geryon (P)										x						
Four-and-Twenty Blackbirds (P)												x		x		
Four Suspects (M)				x												x
Fourth Man (n)					x						x					
Fruitful Sunday (n)						x										
Gate of Baghdad (PP)							x									

	1924: *Poirot Investigates, I:3*	1929: *Partners in Crime, III:2*	1930: *Mysterious Mr. Quin, V:1*	1932: *Thirteen Problems, II:2*	1933: *Hound of Death, XI:1*	1934: *Listerdale Mystery, XI:3*	1934: *Parker Pyne Investigates, IV:1*	1937: *Murder in the Mews, I:17*	1939: *Regatta Mystery, I:20*	1947: *Labours of Hercules, I:26*	1948: *Witness for Prosecution, I:28*	1950: *Three Blind Mice, I:29*	1951: *The Under Dog, I:30*	1960: *Adventures of Xmas Pudding, I:36*	1961: *Double Sin, I:37*	1961: *Thirteen for Luck, I:38*	1965: *Surprise! Surprise! I:40*	1966: *13 Clues for Miss Marple, II:12*	1971: *The Golden Ball, XI:12*
Dressed in Newspaper (TT)		x																	
Hippolyta (P)										x						x			x
he Train (n)					x														x
ll (n)					x														x
's Folly (M)														x	x		x	x	
's Lane (Q)			x																
Got Everything You Want? (PP)							x										x		
eath (M)				x															
Diomedes (P)									x										
Death (n)					x														x
Shiraz (PP)							x												
Lurking Death (TT)		x																	
Your Garden Grow? (P)									x										
l Came About (P)									x										
e of Astarte (M)				x															
s Darkly (n)						x													
e Theft (P)								x											
Gold (M)				x															
earch of a Job (n)					x														x
bery at the Grand Metro- n (P)	x																		
Prime Minister (P)	x																		
lubs (P)													x						
ce (n)				x												x			
r Inheritance (P)														x					
ydra (P)						x													
e Mystery (n)					x														x
(P)	x																		
ctives (Q)											x								

	1924: Poirot Investigates, I:3	1929: Partners in Crime, III:2	1930: Mysterious Mr. Quin, V:1	1932: Thirteen Problems, II:2	1933: Hound of Death, XI:1	1934: Listerdale Mystery, XI:3	1934: Parker Pyne Investigates, IV:1	1937: Murder in the Mews, I:17	1939: Regatta Mystery, I:20	1947: Labours of Hercules, I:26	1948: Witness for Prosecution, I:28	1950: Three Blind Mice, I:29	1951: The Under Dog, I:30	1960: Adventures of Xmas Pudding, I:36	1961: Double Sin, I:37	1961: Thirteen for Luck, I:38
Magnolia Blossom (n)																
Man from the Sea (Q)			x													
Man in the Mist (TT)		x														
Man Who Was No. 16 (TT)		x														
Manhood of Edward Robinson (n)						x										
Market Basing Mystery (P)													x			x
Million Dollar Bond Robbery (P)	x															
Miss Marple Tells a Story (M)									x							
Motive v. Opportunity (M)				x												
Mr. Eastwood's Adventure (n) (American title: Mystery of the Spanish Shawl)						x										
Murder in the Mews (P)								x								
Mystery of Hunter's Lodge (P)	x															
Mystery of the Baghdad Chest (P)									x							
Mystery of the Blue Jar (n)					x											
Mystery of the Spanish Chest (P)														x		
Nemean Lion (P)										x						x
Next to a Dog (n)																
Oracle at Delphi (PP)							x									
Pearl of Price (PP)							x									
Philomel Cottage (n)						x					x					
Plymouth Express (P)													x			
Pot of Tea (TT)		x														
Problem at Pollensa Bay (PP)									x						x	
Problem at Sea (P)									x							
Rajah's Emerald (n)						x										
Red House (TT)		x														
Red Signal (n)					x						x					
Regatta Mystery (PP)									x							x
Sanctuary (M)															x	
Second Gong (P)											x					

Title	1924: Poirot Investigates, I:3	1929: Partners in Crime, III:2	1930: Mysterious Mr. Quin, V:1	1932: Thirteen Problems, II:2	1933: Hound of Death, XI:1	1934: Listerdale Mystery, XI:3	1934: Parker Pyne Investigates, IV:1	1937: Murder in the Mews, I:17	1939: Regatta Mystery, I:20	1947: Labours of Hercules, I:26	1948: Witness for Prosecution, I:28	1950: Three Blind Mice, I:29	1951: The Under Dog, I:30	1960: Adventures of Xmas Pudding, I:36	1961: Double Sin, I:37	1961: Thirteen for Luck, I:38	1965: Surprise! Surprise! I:40	1966: 13 Clues for Miss Marple, II:12	1971: The Golden Ball, XI:12
on the Glass (Q)			x																
the Sky (Q)			x																
Song of Sixpence (n)						x													
(n)					x						x								
the Croupier (Q)			x																
Case of Sir Andrew Carmichael					x														x
Jest (M)												x						x	
lean Birds (P)										x									
ne Plans (P)													x						
dale Mystery (TT)		x																	
ng (n)						x													
asure Murder (M)												x				x		x	
f the Royal Ruby (P)														x					
loor Flat (P)												x					x		
ark of St. Peter (M)				x														x	
at Marsdon Manor (P)	x																		
e at Rhodes (P)								x											
lind Mice (n)												x							
Night Club (M)				x															
able Alibi (TT)		x																	
og (P)														x	x				
Lady (P)	x																		
n the Dark (Q)			x																
Nest (P)															x				
s (n) (American title: Where e's a Will)					x						x						x		
for the Prosecution (n)					x						x						x		
End (Q)			x																
Iris (P)									x										

Index of Characters

The Index of Characters includes all but a small number of the least important of the thousands of characters introduced by the author in her detective and mystery short stories and novels. They are coded to the identification of stories and books used in the master Bibliography so as to allow easier location of a character.

Two points may be noted from this comprehensive index: one, the enormous variety of names used and the remarkably small duplication of them, thus implying a system which for efficiency would rival anything brought by the machine-like Miss Felicity Lemon to her service to Poirot and Pyne; and, second, the great appropriateness of the names used. Both characteristics bespeak the highly experienced writer that Dame Agatha was.

Aarons, Joseph. Theatrical agent. I:5; I:37:a
Abbas Effendi. Tour guide at Petra. IV:1:j
Abbot, __. A local lawyer. VI:3
Abdullah. Expedition helper; Arab. I:13
Abel, __. Police constable. I:37:h
Abercrombie, Col. __. Dentist's patient. I:21
Abernethie, Mrs. Leo (Helen). Widowed sister-in-law of Richard A. I:32
Abernethie, Mrs. Maude. Wife of Timothy A.; sister-in-law of Richard A. I:32
Abernethie, Richard. Recently deceased owner of Enderby Hall. I:32
Abernethie, Timothy. Invalid brother of Richard A. I:32
Achmed. Senior mechanic at Ramat airport. I:35
Ackroyd, Mrs. Cecil. Widowed sister-in-law of Roger A. I:4
Ackroyd, Flora. Niece of Roger A. I:4
Ackroyd, Roger. Wealthy manufacturer. I:4
Adams, Mrs. __. Landlady of Mrs. Chapman. I:21
Adams, Dr. __. Mrs. Pengelly's physician. I:30:f
Adams, Dr. __. Retired physician at Astley Priors. III:1
Adams, Carlotta. Former actress; American. I:8
Afflick, Jackie. Operator of coach tours. II:14

Angkatell, Lucy. Giver of house party; wife of Sir Henry A. I:25
Ankh. Young daughter of Kait. XI:5
___, Anna. Cmdr. Haydock's German helper. III:3
Annesley, Gerard. Husband of Mabelle A. I:38:i
Annesley, Mabelle. Guest of Madge Keeley. I:38:i
___, Annette. Maid in a Soho house. III:1
___, Annie. Maid of the Inglethorpes. I:1
___, Annie. Sheppard housemaid. I:4
___, Annie. Cook to Emily Arundell. I:15
___, Annie. Housemaid to Mrs. Todd. I:30:i
Ansel, ___. Local solicitor. II:7
Anstruther, Mrs. ___. Aunt of Bridget Conway. VI:3
Anstruther, ___. The narrator. XI:1:a
___, Anthea. Tuppence's goddaughter. III:4
Antrobus, Dr. ___. Aide to Parker Pyne; alias: Dr. Claudius
    Constantine. IV:1:f
Appleby, ___. Secretary to Ryland; American. I:5
Appleby, Col. ___. Village bore. II:4
Appledore, ___. Cmdr. Haydock's manservant. III:3
Arbuthnot, Col. ___. Passenger on Orient Express; English. I:9
Arbuthnot, George. Friend of Frankie Derwent; physician. XI:2
Archdale, Betty. Former parlormaid for Lucille Drake. VII:2
Archer, ___. Poacher. II:1
Archer, Mrs. ___. Cleaning woman; mother of poacher. II:1
"Arden, Enoch." Stranger; second cousin of Mrs. Jeremy Cloade;
    real name: Charles Trenton. I:27
Ardingly, David. Friend of Esterbrook; Oxford lecturer in History.
    VIII:1
Argyle, Christina (Tina). Half-caste adopted daughter of Leo A.
    IX:1
Argyle, Hester. Daughter of Leo A. IX:1
Argyle, Leo. Bookish invalid. IX:1
Argyle, Mrs. Leo (Rachel). Murdered wife of Leo A. IX:1
Argyle, Michael (Micky). Son of Leo A. IX:1
Aristides, ___. Rich old man at Fez hotel. XI:8
Aristopoulos, ___. Jeweler in Delphi. IV:1:l
Armstrong, Daisy. Child murdered in New York City. I:9
Armstrong, Dr. Edward George. Harley Street physician. XI:4
Arrichet, Francoise. Housekeeper for Renauld. I:2
Arundell, Charles. Nephew of Emily A.; brother of Theresa A. I:15
Arundell, Emily Harriet Laverton. Old lady in Market Basing. I:15
Arundell, Theresa. Niece of Emily A.; engaged to Dr. Donaldson.
    I:15
Ascanio, Signor Paolo. Visitor to Foscatini; Italian. I:3:j
Ascher, Franz. Ex-waiter; German. I:12
Ascher, Mrs. Franz. Operator of a small tobacco and newspaper

shop. I:12

Ashby, Joan. Dinner guest at Lytcham Close. I:28:i

Ashe, __ . Gardener at Dayas Hall. II:5

Ashley, Diana. Notorious beauty. II:2:b

Askew, Thomas. Inn landlord. VII:1

Astor, Anthony. Playwright (a woman); real name: Muriel Wills. I:10

Astwell, Mrs. __ ("Mother"). Cleaning woman. I:14

Astwell, Lady Nancy. Former actress. I:36:c

Astwell, Sir Reuben. Murdered businessman. I:36:c

Astwell, Victor. Brother and partner of Sir Reuben A. I:36:c

Atkinson, __ . British consular official in Ankara. I:35

Atkinson, Col. __ ("Monty"). Elderly acquaintance of Tommy Beresford. III:5.

Atlas, __ . Newspaper sports reporter. I:26:l

Attenbury, Sir Samuel. Barrister. I:22

__ , August. Renauld gardener. I:2

Austin, Celia. Hospital drug dispenser. I:33

Babbington, Mrs. Margaret. Enthusiastic gardener. I:10

Babbington, Stephen. Local parson. I:10

Bacon, __ . Police inspector. II:8

Badcock, Arthur. Formerly married to Marina Gregg; real name: Alfred Beadle. II:9

Badcock, Mrs. Arthur (Heather). Village housewife. II:9

Badgeworth, Inspector __ . Old acquaintance of Raymond West. II:2:c

Badgworthy, __ . Police inspector. VI:1

Bailey, Donovan. One of quartet locked out of apartment. I:29:f

Bain, Mrs. Mary. Neighbor of Badcocks; a widow. II:9

Baker, __ . London butler to Strange. I:10

Baker, Mrs. Calvin. "Tourist" in Casablanca; American. XI:8

Baker, Mrs. Cherry. Friend and helper to Jane Marple. II:9

Baker, David. Boy friend of Norma Restarick. I:41

Baker, Jim. Helper of Mr. Marsh. I:3:k

Baker, Jim. Husband of Cherry B. II:9

Baker, Richard. Archeologist; English. XI:7

Balderson, __ . Purported member of publishing firm. VI:1

Baldwin, __ . Police superintendent. I:34

Ball, __ . Employee at Black Swan. I:12

Ball, Andrew. Man arrested for ransacking bedroom. I:35

Ballard, __ . Senior partner in jewelry firm. II:11

Balsano, Giuseppe. Waiter in Luxembourg restaurant. VII:2

Banks, Gregory. Assistant in chemist's shop. I:32

Banks, Mrs. Gregory (Susan). Daughter of Gordon Abernethie; niece of Richard A. I:32

Banks, Henry. Important industrialist. I:35

Bantry, Col. Arthur. Owner of Gossington Hall; district magistrate. I:38:f; II:3, 14

Bantry, Mrs. Arthur (Dolly). Wife of Col. Arthur B. I:38:f; II:3, 9, 14

Barber, Mrs. __ . Hostess at a morning coffee. III:5

Barker, Sister __ . Nurse in Carristown hospital. II:13

Barling, Gregory. Financier; friend of Lytcham Roche. I:28:i

Barnaby, Sir George. Husband of murdered woman. V:1:d

Barnaby, Lady Vivien. Murdered wife of Sir George B. V:1:d

Barnard, __ . Father of Elizabeth B.; formerly in ironmongering business. I:12

Barnard, Mrs. __ . Mother of Elizabeth B.; Welsh. I:12

Barnard, Elizabeth. Cafe waitress. I:12

Barnard, Megan. Sister of Elizabeth B. I:12

Barnes, Gen. __ . Old veteran. I:17:d

Barnes, Mrs. __ . Joyce Lambert's landlady. XI:11:o

Barnes, George. Ferry operator. VI:4

Barnes, Reginald. Retired civil servant; dental patient. I:21

Barnes, Will. Ferry operator. VI:4

Barnett, __ . Police inspector. I:36:e

Barrere, __ . Opera singer. XI:3:l

Barrett, Jane. Maid to Lady Tressilian. VI:4

Barron, Dr. __ . Bacteriologist; French. XI:8

Barron, Beatrice. Aunt of Margery Gale. V:1:g

Barrow, Miss __ . Tour passenger. II:13

Barrowby, Amelia. Writer of letter to Poirot. I:20:c

Barry, Maj. __ . Guest at Jolly Roger. I:23

Bartlett, Mrs. __ . Landlady of Joe Ellis. II:2:m

Bartlett, Miss __ . Companion-gardener in St. Mary Mead. II:13

Bartlett, George. Guest at Majestic Hotel. II:3

Barton, Emily. Village spinster. II:4

Barton, Frank. Uncle of Ellie Guteman. XI:9

Barton, George. Husband of Rosemary B. VII:2

Barton, Lady Laura. Old friend of Kingston Bruces. III:2:c

Barton, Mary. Guest at hotel in Las Palmas; English. II:2:h

Barton, Mrs. Rosemary. Sister of Iris Marle; supposedly a suicide. VII:2

Bassington-ffrench, Henry. Husband of Sylvia; a country gentleman. XI:2

Bassington-ffrench, Roger. Brother of Henry B.-f. XI:2

Bassington-ffrench, Mrs. Sylvia. Wife of Henry B.-f. XI:2

Bassington-ffrench, Tommy. Young son of Henry B.-f. XI:2

Bateman, Rupert ("Pongo"). Private secretary to Sir Oswald Coote. VI:2

Bates, Annie. Assistant to the cook. I:36:a

Bateson, Len. Medical student. I:33

Batt, Albert. Assistant to the Beresfords; later a pub proprietor. III:1-5

Bex, M. Lucien. French commissary of police. I:2
Biggs, Mrs. __ . Hostel cleaning woman. I:33
Biggs, Alfred. Page boy in dental building. I:21
Bigland, Ted. Friend of Mary Gerrard; garage worker. I:22
__ , Bill. Scotland Yard informant. I:29:a
Billingsley, __ . London solicitor. II:7
"Bimbo." Danced attendance on Lady Stranleigh. V:1:g
Bindler, Horace. Friend of Raymond West; literary critic. I:36:f
Binton, Diana. Girl with dog smelling of dead fish. VI:4
Birell, Louise. Earlier inamorata of Andrew Restarick. I:41
Bishop, Mrs. Emma. Housekeeper for Mrs. Welman. I:22
Black, Capt. __ . Friend of Maltravers. I:3:b
Blackett, Mrs. __ . Elderly lady visited by Jane Marple. II:13
Blacklock, Charlotte (Lotty). Sister of Letitia B. II:5
Blacklock, Letitia (Letty). Elderly spinster; real name: Charlotte B.
     II:5
Blair, Mrs. Clarence (Suzanne). Well-known society woman. VII:1
Blairgowrie, Duke of. Kidnapper impersonating a nobleman.
     III:2:h
Blake, Miss __ . Junior mistress and teacher at girls' school. I:35
Blake, Basil. Associated with film industry. II:3
Blake, Elvira. Daughter of Bess Sedgwick. II:11
Blake, Meredith. Brother of Philip B. I:24
Blake, Philip. Stockbroker; old friend of Amyas Crale. I:24
Blake, Selina. Mother of Basil B. II:3
Blake, Susan. Good friend of Pamela Lyall. I:17:d
Blake, Mrs. Vera. Involved in former murder case; now missing.
     I:31
Blanche, Mlle. Angele. New French teacher at girls' school. I:35
Bland, __ . Detective inspector. I:34
Bland, Josiah. A contractor. I:39
Bland, Mrs. Josiah (Valerie). Semi-invalid wife of Josiah B. I:39
Blatt, Horace. Guest at Jolly Roger. I:23
Bleibner, __ . Archeologist; American. I:3:f
Bleibner, Rupert. Archeologist's nephew. I:3:f
Blenkinsop, Mrs. __ . Alias of Tuppence during World War II. III:4
Bletchley, Maj. __ . Resident at San Souci Hotel. III:3
Bligh, Gertrude ("Nellie"). Former secretary to Sir Philip Starke.
     III:4
Blore, William Henry. Former C.I.D. man; alias: Davis. XI:4
Blundell, Caleb P. A magnate; American. IV:1:j
Blundell, Carol. Daughter of Caleb B. IV:1:j
Blunt, Alistair. Bank board chairman. I:21
Blunt, Maj. Hector. Big game hunter. I:4
Blunt, Adm. Philip. Cabinet member. XI:10
Bodlicott, Henry. Young son of Mrs. Stephen B. III:5
Bodlicott, Isaac. Village handyman. III:5

Brett, __ . Police doctor. I:17:a

Brewis, Amanda. Secretary-housekeeper to Sir George Stubbs. I:34

Brewster, __ . Nurse-attendant to elder Denman. II:2:f

Brewster, Emily. Athletic spinster. I:23

Brewster, Jim. Young conspirator. XI:10

Brewster, Lola. Movie actress; once married to Marina Gregg's third husband; American. II:9

Brice-Woodworth, Patricia. At adjoining restaurant table to Barton party. VII:2

__ , Bridget. Young cousin of Colin Lacey. I:36:a

Briggs, __ . Police constable. I:12

Briggs, __ . Old head gardener at girls' school. I:35

Bristow, Frank. Young artist. V:1:i

Broadribb, James. London solicitor. II:13

"Brown, __ ." Mastermind behind revolutionary plot. III:1

Brown, Geraldine. Little girl in Wilbraham Crescent. I:39

Brown, Jimmy. Young boy, observer of drowning. II:2:m

Brown, Laurence. Former tutor to Leonides grandchildren. XI:6

Brown, Lynette. Marina Gregg's backup in film role. II:9

Browne, Anthony. Suitor of Iris Marle; formerly in jail as Tony Morelli. VII:2

Brun, Mlle. Genevieve. French governess to younger Caterham daughters. VI:1

Bryant, Dr. Roger James. Airplane passenger. I:11

Buckle, Mrs. __ . Mother of Marlene B. I:43

Buckle, Doris. Dairy employee. I:19

Buckle, Marlene. Clerk in chemist's shop. I:43

Buckley, Rev. Giles. Father of Maggie B. I:7

Buckley, Maggie (Magdala). Cousin of Nick B. I:7

Buckley, Miss Nick (Magdala). Owner of End House. I:7

Bullard, Louisa. Former housemaid to Sir George Barnaby. V:1:d

Bulmer, Sir Edwin. Barrister; a K.C. I:22

Bulstrode, Honoria. Owner and headmistress of Meadowbrook School. I:35

Bunner, Dora. Old school chum of Letty Blacklock. II:5

Burch, Joe. Husband of Bessie B. I:31

Burch, Mrs. Joe (Bessie). Niece of Mrs. McGinty. I:31

Burgess, Miss __ . Secretary to Dr. Roberts. I:14

Burgess, William. Manservant to Maj. Rich. I:36:b

Burnaby, Maj. John Edward. Retired officer. X:1

Burns, Charlie. Shipping clerk; fiancé of Gillian West. I:38:h

Burrows, Godfrey. Secretary to Sir Gervase Chevenix-Gore. I:17:c

Burshaw, Miss __ . Assistant to Miss Pope. I:26:j

Burt, __ . U.S. Secret Service agent. I:3:c

Burton, Dr. __ . Fellow of All Souls College. I:26:a

Burton, Dr. __ . Physician at Thurnly. III:2:e

Burton, Jerry. The narrator; house renter from Emily Barton. II:4

Burton, Joanna. Sister of narrator. II:4

Burton-Cox, Mrs. __ . Luncheon discussant with Ariadne Oliver. I:43

Burton-Cox, Desmond. Adopted son of Mrs. B.-C.; natural son of Kathleen Fenn, actress. I:43

Bury, Col. Edward (Ned). Old friend of Chevenix-Gore family. I:17:c

Butler, Henry T. Bus tour passenger with wife; American. II:13

Butler, Mrs. Judith. Friend of Ariadne Oliver. I:42

Butler, Miranda. Daughter of Mrs. Judith B. I:42

Butt, Mrs. __ . Resident of Chipping Cleghorn. II:5

Butt, Johnnie. Paper delivery boy in Chipping Cleghorn. II:5

Cabot, Elmer. Guest at hotel with wife. II:11

Cade, Anthony. Tour director. VI:1

Calder, Alice. Secret wife of Ali. I:35

Calder, Allen. Son of Alice C. I:35

Caldicott, Mrs. __ . Tour member. VI:1

Campbell, Mrs. __ . Jennifer Sutcliffe's godmother. I:35

Campbell, Inspector __ . Scotland Yard official. II:11

Campion, Lord Edward. Owner of beach cabana. XI:3:k

Capel, Derek. Former owner of Royston. V:1:a

Capstick, Nurse __ . Nurse to Lady Clarke. I:12

Carbury, Col. __ . Police official. I:18

Cardew Trench, Mrs. __ . Guest at Tio Hotel. XI:7

Cardiff, Peter. Artist. I:41

Cardwell, Susan. Guest at Hamborough Close; friend of Hugo Trent. I:17:c

Carey, Richard. Architect with Leidner expedition. I:13

Carlile, __ . Private secretary to Lord Mayfield. I:17:b

Carlisle, Elinor. Niece of Mrs. Welman. I:22

Carlton-Sandways, Lady Veronica. Mother of twins at girls' school. I:35

Carlton-Smith, Naomi. Guest at Corsican hotel; artist; English. V:1:f

Carmichael, Lady __ . Neighborhood gossip monger. I:26:i

Carmichael, Lady __ . Second wife of Sir William C. XI:1:i

Carmichael, Andrew (or Arthur). A baronet. XI:11:l (or XI:l:i)

Carmichael, Henry. British agent; alias: Walter Williams. XI:7

Carmichael, William. Senior partner in London law firm. I:16

Carmody, Peter. Son of Adelaide Jefferson by first husband. II:3

Carnaby, Amy. Companion to Lady Hoggin. I:26:b, k.

Carnaby, Emily. Sister of Amy C. I:26:b

Carpenter, Mrs. __ . Friend of Elvira Blake. II:11

Carpenter, Mrs. Adelaide. Village widow. II:2:k

Carpenter, Dickie. Former fiancé of Esther Lawes. XI:1:d

Carpenter, Guy. Rich man interested in politics. I:31

Carpenter, Mrs. Guy (Eve). Wife of Guy C.; formerly: Mrs. Selkirk. I:31

Carr, Lady Esther. Recluse at Shiraz; real name: Muriel King. IV:1:i

Carraway, Mrs. __ . Patient at Sunny Ridge home. III:4

Carrège, M. __ . Juge d'Instruction at Nice. I:6

Carrington, Sir George. Air Marshal. I:17:b

Carrington, Lady Julia. Guest at party. I:17:b

Carrington, Reggie. Son of Lady Julia C. I:17:b

Carrington, Mrs. Rupert (Flossie). Daughter of Ebenezer Halliday. I:30:b

Carroll, Miss __ . Secretary to Lord Edgware. I:8

Carruthers, Nurse __ . Nurse to Emily Arundell. I:15

Carruthers, Miss __ . Guest at same hotel with the Rhodes. I:20:f

Carslake, Alan. Younger brother of Neil C. I:20:h

Carslake, Neil. Narrator's best friend. I:20:h

Carslake, Sylvia. Sister of Neil C. I:20:h

Carstairs, Alan. Big game hunter; Canadian; *see* Alex Pritchard. VII:1

Carstairs. Dr. Edward. Author-narrator of diary. XI:1:i

Carstairs, Hon. Julia. Old friend of Ariadne Oliver. I:43

Carter, Col. __ . Village resident. I:4

Carter, __ . Police superintendent for Sussex. I:12

Carter, __ . "Detective sergeant." XI:3:i

Carter, A. Government official; real name: Lord Easthampton. III:1-3

Carter, Lucy. Daughter of Harry C., saloon keeper. VI:3

Carter, Stephen. In diplomatic service. I:20:e

Carton, L.B. Man electrocuted in subway; husband of Nadina. VII:1

Carton, Frank. Insurance clerk; friend of Gladys Nevill I:21

Cartwright, Dr. __ . Physician at Market Basing. VI:1-2

Cartwright, Sir Charles. Actor. I:10

Carver, Dr. __ . World-renowned archeologist. IV:1:j

Cary, Frances. Roommate of Norma Restarick; daughter of a country solicitor. I:41

Casey, Mrs. __ . Landlady of Culver Street house. I:29:a

Casey, Patrick. A cat burglar. I:26:l

Caspar, __ . Tour passenger. II:13

Caspearo, Sra. de. Hotel guest; Venezuelan. II:10

Cassell, Dr. __ . Small town physician. VI:2

Casson, Mrs. __ . A medium. V:1:g

Castle, Mrs. __ . Owner of Jolly Roger Hotel. I:23

Castleton, Harry. Suspected former husband of Merlina Rival. I:39

Caterham. Lord. Ninth marquis; name: Clement Edward Alistair Brent. VI:1-2

Caux, M. __ . Commissary of police at Nice. I:6

Christow, Dr. John. House guest of Lucy Angkatell. I:25
Christow, Mrs. John (Gerda). Wife of John C. I:25
Christow, Terence. Young son of Dr. C. I:25
Chudleigh, Mrs. Rose. Templeton cook. VII:1
Church, Miss ___. Aunt of Amy Gibbs. VI:3
Church, Beatrice. Housemaid to Sir Bartholomew Strange. I:10
"Cinderella." Wife of Capt. Hastings in Argentina. I:5
Clancy, Daniel Michael. Plane passenger; detective-story writer.
    I:11.
Clapperton, "Col." John. Bogus war hero. I:20:i
Clapperton, Mrs. John (Adeline). Wife of "Col." C. I:20:i
___, Clara. Maid to Mrs. Price-Ridley. I:29:d
Clark, Miss ___. Companion to Mrs. Templeton. I:5
Clark, Miss ___. Companion to Mrs. Jones. II:2:a
Clark, Dr. Campbell. Mental specialist. I:28:c
Clark, Jennifer. Barmaid at Three Crowns. II:4
Clarke, Sir Carmichael. Man murdered at Churston; well-known
    throat specialist. I:12
Clarke, Lady Charlotte. Wife of Sir Carmichael C; dying of cancer.
    I:12
Clarke, Franklin. Brother of Sir Carmichael C. I:12
___, Mlle. Claude. Assistant to Mme. Olivier. I:5
Claygate, Lady ___. Neighbor of the Lemesuriers. I:30:e
Claythorne, Vera Elizabeth. Former governess. XI:4
Clayton, Alice. Maid to Lady Stranleigh. V:1:g
Clayton, Arnold. Treasury Department official. I:36:b
Clayton, Mrs. Arnold (Margharita). Wife of Arnold C. I:36:b
Clayton, Mrs. Elsie. Hotel guest; daughter of Mrs. Rice. I:26:g
Clayton, Gerald. British consul general at Basrah. XI:7
Clayton, Mrs. Gerald. Wife of consul general. XI:7
Clayton, Philip. "Husband" of Elsie C. I:26:g
Cleat, Mrs. ___. Village "witch." II:4
Cleaver, Sir William. A justice. VI:4
Cleckheaton, Lady Matilda. Great-aunt of Nye. XI:10
Clegg, Miss ___. Housekeeper to Walter Protheroe. I:30:d
Clegg, Mrs. Emmeline. Friend of Amy Carnaby. I:26:k
Clegg, Freda. Girl rescued by Maj. Wilbraham. IV:1:b
Clegg, Joe. Second husband of Maureen C. IX:1
Clegg, Mrs. Joe (Maureen). Widow of Jacko Argyle; movie theater
    usher. IX:1
Clement, Dennis. Nephew of vicar. II:1
Clement, Griselda. Wife of vicar. II:1, 3
Clement, Leonard. Vicar at St. Mary Mead. II:1, 3
Cleveland, Jane. Girl looking for job. XI:3:g
Cleveland, Mortimer. Driver of car near Dinsmead house. XI:1:a
Cleves, Diana. Adopted daughter of Lytcham Roches. I:28:i
Clipp, Hamilton. Husband of Mrs. C. XI:7

Clipp, Mrs. Hamilton. Passenger to Baghdad; American. XI:7

Clithering, Sir Henry. Ex-Commissioner of Scotland Yard. I:38:f; II:2:a, h, i, j; II:3, 5

Cloade, Gordon. Killed in recent bomb blast. I:27

Cloade, Mrs. Gordon (Rosaleen). Widow of Gordon C.; formerly wife of Robert Underhay; real name: Eileen Corrigan. I:27

Cloade, Jeremy. Brother of Gordon C. I:27

Cloade, Mrs. Jeremy (Frances). Daughter of Lord Edward Trenton. I:27

Cloade, Dr. Lionel. Younger brother of Gordon C. I:27

Cloade, Mrs. Lionel (Katharine; Kathie). Wife of Dr. C; a spiritualist I:27

Cloade, Rowley (Rowland). Nephew of Gordon C.; cousin and fiancé of Lynn Marchmont. I:27

Clode, Chris (Christobel). Orphaned granddaughter of Simon C.; deceased. II:2:e

Clode, George. Nephew of Simon C. II:2:e

Clode, Mary. Niece of Simon C. II:2:e

Clode, Simon. Wealthy semi-invalid. II:2:e

Clydesly, __ . Scotland Yard agent. III:2:g

Cobb, __ . Police sergeant. I:33

Cobb, __ . Official of Harchester Art Galleries. V:1:i

Cocker, Mrs. __ . Cook for the Reeds. II:14

Cocker, Doris. Under housemaid at Melfort Abbey. I:10

Cocoa, Mrs. __ . *See* Moody, Mrs. Elizabeth. III:4

Coggins, __ . Accomplice of "Dymchurch." III:2:d

Cohen, Sir Herman. Name Jane Helier used for owner of bungalow. II:2:l

Coin, M. __ . Minister for Home Affairs. XI:10

Coker, Mrs. __ . Elderly lady who lived with Loraine Wade. VI:2

Cole, __ . Member of religious sect. I:26:k

Cole, Miss __ . Proprietor of Mitre Hotel. I:36:c

Cole, Elizabeth. Lodger at Styles. I:44

Coleman, William. New Member of Leidner expedition; English. I:13

Coles, Doris. Guest of Madge Keeley. I:38:i

Colgate, Inspector __ . Police officer. I:23

Collier, Beryl. Secretary to Dr. Christow. I:25.

Collins, Miss __ . Secretary to Mr. Waverly. I:29:g

Collodon, Miss __ . Researcher for Tommy. III:5

Combeau, Pierre. Old friend of Poirot. I:5

Comstock, __ . Scotland Yard official. II:11

Conneau, Georges. A lover of Jeanne Beraldy. I:2

Conrad, Mrs. __ . London society lady. I:30:h

__ , Conrad. Plugugly who conked Tommy in Soho house. III:1

Constantine, Dr. __ . Physician on Orient Express; Greek. I:9

Conway, Bridget. Cousin of Jimmie Lorrimer; secretary and fiancee of Lord Easterfield. VI:3

Conway, Sir George. Home Secretary. I:26:f

Conway, Sir Richard. Soldier, traveler, and sportsman. V:1:a

Cooke, Miss __. Tour passenger. II:13

Coombe, Alicia. Proprietor of dressmaker's shop. I:37:d

Coote, Lady Maria. Mistress of Chimneys estate. VI:2

Coote, Sir Oswald. Owner of Chimneys; steel manufacturer. VI:2

Cope, Jefferson. Old friend of Mrs. Nadine Boynton; American. I:18

Copes, Mrs. __. Col. Pikeaway's landlady. III:5

Copleigh, Mrs. __. Village gossip. III:4

Copleigh, George. Husband of Mrs. C. III:4

Copling, Nurse __. Attendant on Mrs. George Pritchard. I:38:f

Coppins, Mrs. __. Owner of house visited by priest. VIII:1

Cornelly, Lord __. Rich peer who gave MacWhirter a job. VI:4

Corner, Sir Montagu. Dinner host. I:8

Cornish, Frank. Police sergeant at St. Mary Mead. II:8-9

Cornworthy, Hugo. Private secretary of Benedict Farley. I:36:e

Corrigan, Dr. James. Police doctor. VIII:1

Corrigan, "Ginger." Guest at party with Rhoda Despard. VIII:1

Cortman, Mrs. Mildred Jean (Milly). Wife of American ambassador; alias: Juanita. XI:10

Cortman, Sam. American ambassador. XI:10

Cosdon, Anthony. Companion of Mr. Satterthwaite. V:1:k

Cottrell, Frank. Police sergeant. I:34

Courtenay, Coco. An actress. I:30:c

Courtland, Mrs. Janice. Involved in former murder case; now missing. I:31

Cowan, __. Business manager to Mme. Nazorkoff. XI:3:l

Cowley, Archdeacon __. Father of Tuppence. III:1

Crabtree, Mrs. __. Bedridden patient of Dr. Christow. I:25

Crabtree, Lily. Great-aunt of Magdalen Vaughan. XI:3:d

Crabtree, William. Nephew of Lily Crabtree. XI:3:d

Crabtree, Mrs. William (Emily). Wife of William C. XI:3:d

Crackenthorpe, Alfred. Blacksheep son of Luther C. II:8

Crackenthorpe, Cedric. Son of Luther C.; bohemian painter. II:8

Crackenthorpe, Emma. Daughter of Luther C. II:8

Crackenthorpe, Harold. Son of Luther C. II:8

Crackenthorpe, Luther. Cantankerous skinflint. II:8

Craddock, Mrs. __. Former employer of Elsie Batt. I:14

Craddock, Dermott. Scotland Yard inspector; godson of Clithering. I:37:h; II:5, 8-9

Craig, Dr. Donald. Fiancé of Hester Argyle. IX:1

Crale, Amyas. Artist. I:24

Crale, Mrs. Caroline (née Spalding). Mother of Carla Lemarchant. I:24

Cram, Gladys. Secretary to Dr. Stone. II:1

Dacre, Mrs. Denis (Margery). Wife of Capt. Denis D. II:2:d
Dacre, Mrs. Joyce. Second wife of Capt. Denis D. II:2:d
Dacres, Mrs. Cynthia. Owner of dressmaking shop. I:10
Dacres, Capt. Freddie. Horse racing devotee. I:10
Dakin, __ . Oil company official. XI:7
Dale, Elsie. Ackroyd housemaid. I:4
Dale, Sylvia. Daughter of the village doctor. V:1:d
Dalehouse, Harry. Nephew of Lytcham Roche. I:28:i
Danby, Alison. Aunt of Gwenda Reed. II:14
Dane Calthrop, Caleb. Elderly vicar. II:4; VIII:1
Dane Calthrop, Mrs. (Maude). Vicar's wife. II:4; VIII:1
Daniels, Capt. __ . Secretary to Prime Minister. I:3:h
Daniels, __ . Lawyer. VI:4
Darnley, Rosamund. Fashionable dressmaker. I:23
Darrell, Claud. Former actor. I:5
Darrell, Richard. Husband of Theodora D. XI:11:n
Darrell, Mrs. Richard (Theodora). Beloved by Vincent Easton.
    XI:11:n
Dashwood, Everitt. Newspaper reporter. I:26:f
Daubreuil, Mme. __ . Neighbor of the Renaulds; real name: Jeanne
    Beroldy. I:2
Daubreuil, Mlle. Daughter of Mme. D. I:2
Daubreuil, Raoul. Engineer; fiancé of Simone. I:37:g
Davenheim, __ . Banker. I:3:i
Daventry, __ . Friend of Dr. Graham. II:10
Daventry, Vera. Girl guest at Chimneys. VI:2
David, Lucy. Cook for Simon Clode. II:2:e
Davidson, Dr. __ . Divisional surgeon for Scotland Yard. I:14
Davidson, Dr. __ . Coroner at Staverley. VII:1
Davidson, Chris. Young actor. I:30:c
Davidson, Mrs. Chris. Actor's wife. I:30:c
Daviloff, Sonia. Niece of Savaronoff. I:5
Davis, __ . Police inspector. I:4
Davis, __ . Absconding bank employee. I:30:i
Davis, Mrs. __ . Dying woman at Coppin house. VIII:1
Davis, __ . Nurse to Mrs. Gardner. X:1
"Davis, __ ." Invitee to Indian Island; South African. XI:4
Davis, Albert. Second steward on plane. I:11
Davis, Giles. Operator of Monkswell Manor Guest House. I:29:a
Davis, Mrs. Giles (Molly). Wife of Giles D. I:29:a
Davy, Fred. A chief inspector at Scotland Yard. II:11
Dawes, Rhoda. Friend of Miss Meredith. I:14
Deane, Molly. Fiancée of Harrison. I:37:b
Deane, Monica. Resident in a house with poltergeists. III:2:n
Deaves, George. Valet to Ryland. I:5
de Bellefort, Jacqueline. Friend of Linnet Ridgeway. I:16
Debenham, Mary Hermione. English governess. I:9

___, Dorothy. Housemaid for the Denmans. II:2:f

Dortheimer, ___. Music patron. I:8

Dortheimer, Mrs. ___. Wife of Mr. D. I:8

Dortheimer, Rachel. Daughter of Mr. D. I:8

Dove, Mary. Housekeeper. II:7

Dover, ___. Police constable at Andover. I:12

Downes, Roger Emmanuel. Master at Highfield School for boys. I:12

Doyle, Simon. Fiancé of Jacqueline de Bellefort; later married Linnett Ridgeway. I:16

Drage, Lady Cynthia. Friend of Mr. Satterthwaite. V:1:b

Dragomiroff, Princess Natalia. Elderly aristocrat; Russian. I:9

Drake, Allen. Partner of Thomas Royde. VI:4

Drake, Mrs. Hugo (Rowena). Hostess at party. I:42

Drake, Mrs. Lucille. Widowed aunt of Iris Marle. VII:2

Drake, Una. Girl whom Jones fell for; Australian. I:38:l

Drake, Vera. Twin sister of Una D. I:38:l

Drake, Victor. Blacksheep son of Lucille D. VII:2

Draper, Mrs. Mary (neé Riley). Aunt of Mary Gerrard; alias: Jessie Hopkins. I:22

Drewitt, ___. Police inspector at St. Mary Mead. II:2:m

Driver, ___. Police inspector. XI:3:i

Driver, Jenny. Hat shop proprietor. I:8

Drouet, ___. Swiss police inspector; *see* Gustave. I:26:e

Drower, Mary. Parlormaid; niece of Mrs. Ascher. I:12

Dubois, Vivian Edward. Escort of Adele Fortescue. II:7

Dubosc, Lt. ___. French officer at Aleppo. I:9

Dubosc, Col. ___. Gallant officer on leave from Syria; French. IV:1:j

Duke, ___. Buyer of last cottage at Sittaford House. X:1

Dundas, George. Nephew of Ephraim Leadbetter. XI:3:j

Dunn, Eliza. Cook for Mrs. Todd. I:30:i

Dupont, Armand. Plane passenger; archeologist; French. I:11

Dupont, Jean. Plane passenger; archeologist; French. I:11

Duguesclin, Quentin. Man who disappeared mysteriously; Canadian. I:39

Durand, Dr. ___. Physician; French. I:2

Durand, Sir George. Lawyer. I:28:c

Durrance, ___. Operator of village photography shop. III:5

Durrant, Amy. Guest at hotel in Las Palmas; English. II:2:h

Durrant, Mary. Niece of antique shop owner. I:37:a

Durrant, Philip. Son-in-law of Leo Argyle; a polio victim. IX:1

Durrant, Mrs. Philip (Mary; Polly). Daughter of Leo Argyle. IX:1

Duveen, Bella. Jack Renauld's inamorata. I:2

___, Edna. Maid to Jane Marple. I:29:d

___, Edna. Assistant to Mrs. Sweetman. I:31

Edwards, ___. Valet to Conway Jefferson. II:3

Edwards, Constable ___. Police stenographer. II:5

Egerton, Richard. Lawyer. II:11

Elford, ___. Lawyer at Chipping Somerton. VII:1

Elford, Florence. Maid to Emily Barton. II:4

___, Elise. Maid to Simone. I:37:g

___, Elise. Maid to Lady Laura Barton; French. III:2:c

___, Elise. Maid to Virginia Revel. VI:1

___, Elise. Maid to Mme. Nazorkoff. XI:3:l

___, Elizabeth. Maid to Mrs. Harter. I:28:e

___, Ellen. Maid to Emily Arundell. I:15

___, Ellen. Maid to Mrs. Honeycott. III:2:i

Ellerby, Maj. ___. Former employee of Parker. I:4

Elliot, Mrs. ___. Next-door neighbor of Mrs. McGinty. I:31

Elliot, Lady Noreen. Girl with diamond necklace. XI:3:e

Ellis, ___. Maid to Jane Wilkinson. I:8

Ellis, Mrs. ___. Cook for the Sutcliffes. I:35

Ellis, Miss ___. Private secretary to Harold Crackenthorpe. II:8

Ellis, Jim. Common-law husband of Victoria Johnson. II:10

Ellis, Joe. Carpenter; local beau of Rose Emmott. II:2:m

Ellis, John. Butler to Strange. I:10

Ellis, Lou. Girl who fought at restaurant. VIII:1

Ellsworthy, ___. Owner of antique shop. VI:3

___, Elspeth. Forewoman in dressmaker's shop. I:37:d

Elvary, Mme. ___. A spiritualist medium. I:27

el Ziyara, Sheikh Hussein. Arab V.I.P. XI:7

___, Emily. Maid to Mrs. Waynflete. VI:3

___, Emily. Servant to the Beddingfelds. VII:1

Emlyn, Miss ___. A headmistress. I:42

Emmott, David. Member of Leidner expedition; American. I:13

Emmott, Doris. Kitchen maid to the Angkatells. I:25

Emmott, Rose. Daughter of village tavern keeper. II:2:m

Emmott, Tom. Father of Rose E. II:2:m

Emory, Mrs. ___. Daily woman for the Burtons. II:4

Enderby, Charles. Newspaper reporter. X:1

Endicott, ___. Lawyer. I:33

Entwhistle, ___. Abernethie lawyer. I:32

Entwhistle, Miss ___. Sister of lawyer. I:32

Ericsson, Torquil. Physicist; Norwegian. XI:8

Erskine, Maj. Richard. Former Dillmouth resident. II:14

Erskine, Mrs. Richard (Janet). Wife of Richard E. II:14

Farrell, __ . Detective inspector. XI:3:g

Faulkener, Jimmie. One of quartet locked out of apartment. I:29:f

Faulkener, Capt. Jimmie. Young socialite gambler. III:2:j

Faulkener, Leslie. Playwright. II:2:l

Faussett, Dr. __ . Physician attending Amyas Crale. I:24

__ , Félicie. Maid in Déroulard house. I:3:n

Fellows-Brown, Mrs. __ . Patron of dressmaker's shop. I:37:d

Fenn, Ardwyck. TV and film magnate. II:7

Ferguson, __ . Hippie on Nile trip; real name: Lord Dawlish. I:16

Ferguson, Dr. __ . Village physician. I:42

__ , Fernando. Head waiter at hotel. II:10

Ferrarez, Carmen. Former convent resident. XI:3:i

Ferrars, Mrs. Ashley. Patient of Dr. Sheppard. I:4

Ferrier, Lesley. Law firm employee. I:42

Ferrier, Edward. Prime Minister; son-in-law of John Hammett. I:26:f

Ferrier, Mrs. Edward. Wife of Prime Minister. I:26:f

Finch, Mrs. __ . Swettenham maid. II:5

Finch, Sally. Student at hostel; American. I:33

Findeyson, Mrs. __ . Former occupant of Reeds' house. II:14

Finn, Jane. Orphan girl who took packet on *Lusitania*; American. III:1

Finney, Maj. __ . Chief Constable of police. IX:1

Fish, Hiram P. Guest at Chimneys; American. VI:1

Fitzroy, __ . Secretary to Lord Alloway. I:30:h

Fitzwilliam, Luke. Recently retired police officer in Asia. VI:3

Flavelle, Hippolyte. Valet to de la Roche. I:6

Flavelle, Marie. Wife of Hippolyte F.; cook. I:6

Fleetwood, __ . Crewman on Nile ship. I:16

Flemming, __ . Beddingfeld solicitor. VII:1

Flemming, Mrs. __ . Wife of solicitor. VII:1

Fletcher, Sgt. __ . Police sergeant at Chipping Cleghorn. I:31; II:5

Fletcher, Agnes. Cook for Miss Morley. I:21

Fletcher, Nat. Nephew of Miss Greenshaw. I:36:f

__ , Florence. Former maid of Jane Marple. II:8

Fogg, Quentin. A K.C. I:24

Folliat, Mrs. Amy. Widow; original owner of manor. I:34

Folliott, Mrs. __ . Former employer of Ursula Bourne. I:4

Forbes, Gen. __ . Ship passenger. I:20:i

Forbes, Ogilvie. Lawyer for Chevenix-Gore family. I:17:c

Ford, Monica. Inamorata of Hugo Charnley. V:1:i

Fortescue, Elaine. Daughter of Rex F. by first wife. II:7

Fortescue, Lancelot ("Lance"). Younger son of Rex F. II:7

Fortescue, Mrs. Lancelot ("Pat"). Wife of Lancelot F. II:7

Fortescue, Percival ("Val"). Older son of Rex F. II:7

Fortescue, Mrs. Percival (Jennifer). Wife of Percival F.; former nurse. II:7

Fortescue, Rex. Head of Consolidated Investment Trust. II:7

Fortescue, Mrs. Rex (Adele). Young second wife of Rex F.; former manicurist. II:7

Foscarelli, Antonio. Passenger on Orient Express. I:9

Foscatini, Count __. Italian nobleman. I:3:j

Foster, __. Gardener for the Reeds. II:14

Fournier, M. __. Official of French Sûreté. I:11

Fowler, Mrs. __. Next-door neighbor of Mrs. Ascher. I:12

Fox, Sybil. Employee in dressmaking shop. I:37:d

__, François. Servant of M. Déroulard. I:3:n

Franklin, Dr. John. Lodger at Styles; scientist. I:44

Franklin, Mrs. John (Barbara). Wife of Dr. F. I:44

"Franz Joseph." Young protegé of Gräfin Charlotte; real name: Karl Aguileros. XI:10

Fraser, Donald. Fiancé of Elizabeth Barnard. I:12

__, Fred. Bar tender at Peacock Arms. I:39

Freemantle, Freddie. Escaped convict. X:1

French, Emily. Elderly lady befriended by Leonard Vole. I:28:c

__, Frieda. Maid to Mrs. Carpenter. I:31

Frobisher, Col. George. Oldest friend of Adm. Chandler. I:26:h

Fullerton, Jeremy. Lawyer. I:42

Fullerton, Lavinia. Gentle village lady. VI:3

Gabler, __. A realtor. I:15

Gaigh, Elizabeth. Girl hiding in train. XI:3:c

Gaitskill, __. Leonides lawyer. XI:6

Galbraith, Dr. __. Bishop of Cromer. II:6

Galbraith, __. Retired real estate agent. II:14

Galbraith, Jim. Newspaper reporter. II:9

Gale, Margery. Daughter of Lady Stranleigh. V:1:g

Gale, Norman. Plane passenger; dentist; real name: James Richards. I:11

Gamboll. Lily. Involved in former murder case; now missing. I:31

Ganett. Miss __. Village gossip. I:4

Gapp, Flossie. Real name of Mrs. Merlina Rival, q.v. I:39

Garcia, Dr. Alan. Home Office analyst. I:22; I:26:c

Gardener, Odell C. Tourist; American. I:23

Gardener, Mrs. Odell (Carrie). Wife of Odell G. I:23

Gardiner, John. Secretary to Hugo Lemesurier. I:30:e

Gardner, Mrs. __. Farmwife. IV:1:f

Gardner, Brian. Nephew of Trevelyan. X:1

Gardner, Jennifer. Sister of Capt. Trevelyan. X:1

Gardner, Robert. Invalid husband of Jennifer G. X:1

Garfield, Michael. Landscape architect. I:42

Garfield, Ronald. Nephew of Miss Percehouse. X:1

Garnett, Patricia. Girl locked out of apartment. I:29:f

Garrod, Philip. Research chemist. II:2:e

Garrod, Mrs. Philip (Grace). Wife of Philip G.; niece of Simon Clode. II:2:e

Garroway, Chief Supt. __. Retired police inspector. I:43

Gascoigne, Anthony. Twin brother of Henry G. I:36:d

Gascoigne, Henry. Eccentric diner at Galant Endeavour restaurant. I:36:d

Gaskell, Mark. Husband of Rosamund Jefferson. II:3

Gaunt, Emma. Longtime servant of Simon Clode. II:2:e

__. Georges. Concierge at Mme. Giselle's apartment. I:11

Gerahty, Mrs. __. Priest's housekeeper. VIII:1

Gerard, Alec. Young playwright. V:1:f

Gerard, Dr. Theodore. Physician; French. I:18

Gerard, Ted. Young man at St. Mary Mead. I:29:c

__, Geronimo. Servant at hostel; Italian. I:33

Gerrard, Bob. Supposed father of Mary G.; lodgekeeper. I:22

Gerrard, Mary. Protegé of Mrs. Welman. I:22

Gibbons, Mrs. __. School cook. I:35

Gibbs, Amy. Former housemaid at Ashe Hall. VI:3

Gilchrist, __. Companion-housekeeper of Cora Lansquenet. I:32

Gilchrist, Dr. Maurice. Personal physician to Marina Gregg. II:9

Giles, Dr. __. Physician at Market Basing. I:30:d

Giles, __. Church sexton. VI:3

Ginch, Miss __. Symmington's law clerk. II:4

Giraud, M. __. Detective from Paris Sûreté. I:2

Gisell, Mme. __. Parisian money lender; passport name: Marie Angelique Morisot. I:11

__, Giuseppe. Butler for Marina Gregg. II:9

__, Gladdie. Protheroe kitchen maid. II:1

__, Gladys. Hairdresser at Antoine's. I:11

__, Gladys. Maid to Miss Leatheran. I:26:c

__, Gladys. Third housemaid to Astwells. I:36:c

__, Gladys. Former maid to Jane Marple. I:37:h

Glen, Inspector __. Police official at Andover. I:12

Glen, Aspasia. Stage impersonator; real name: Monica Ford. V:1:i

Glen, Gilda. Prominent actress. III:2:i

Glover, __. Butler to Sir Arthur Hayward. XI:6

Glydr, Maj. Boris. Ostensible cousin of Betterton's first wife, Elsa. XI:8

Glynne, Mrs. Lavinia. Woman Jane Marple met on tour. II:13

Goby, __. Investigator for Poirot. I:6; I:32; I:41-43.

Goedler, Randall. Financier; real name: Dmitri Stamfordis. II:5

Goedler, Mrs. Randall (Belle). Wealthy invalid widow of Randall G. II:5

Goedler, Sonia. Sister of Randall G.; wife of Dmitri Stamfordis. II:5

Gold, Douglas Cameron. Visitor at Rhodes. I:17:d

Green, Cyril. Small boy who saw the strange car after the murder. IX:1

Greene, Netta. Jane Helier's understudy. II:2:1

Greenholtz, __ . Employer of Victoria Jones. XI:7

Greenshaw, Katherine Dorothy. Owner of quaint house. I:36:f

Greenshaw, Laura. Sister of Katherine G. I:36:f

Greenshaw, Nettie. Sister of Katherine G. I:36:f

Greer, Elsa. Manufacturer's daughter; had been in love with Amyas Crale; present name: Lady Dittisham. I:24

Gregg, Betty. Modern girl vacationing on Majorca; fiancée of Basil Chester. I:20:d

Gregg, Ernie. Young Stonygates inmate. II:6

Gregg, Marina. Movie star. II:9

__ , Gretel. Maid to Mrs. McNaughton; Danish. I:39

Grey, __ . Berkshire detective sergeant. I:26:c

Grey, Jane. Plane passenger; hairdresser. I:11

Grey, Katherine. Former companion to Mrs. Jane Harfield. I:6

Grey, Mary. Joanna's London dressmaker. II:4

Grey, Thora. Secretary to Sir Carmichael Clarke. I:12

Grey, Thyrza. Owner of Pale Horse, former pub. VIII:1

Griffin, Mrs. Winifred. Elderly tea hostess to Tuppence. III:5

Griffith, Miss __ . Head typist for Consolidated Investment Trust. II:7

Griffith, Aimée. Sister of Dr. G. II:4

Griffith, Dr. Owen. Physician in Lymstock. II:4

Griffiths, __ . Village doctor. I:37:h

__ , Griselda. Vicar's wife at St. Mary Mead; friend of Jane Marple. II:8

Grosier, Maître __ . Counsel for Jack Renauld. I:2

Grosjean, M. __ . Leader of an international group. XI:10

Grosvenor, Irene. Personal secretary to Fortescue. II:7

Groves, Mrs. __ . Cleaning woman in dress shop. I:37:d

Gudgeon, __ . Butler to the Angkatells. I:25

Gulbrandsen, Christian. Stepson of Carrie Louise Serrocold. II:6

__ , Gustave. Waiter at Swiss mountain resort; "real" name: Drouet. I:26:e

Guteman, Ellie. *See* Rogers, Mrs. Michael. XI:9

Guthrie, Alexander. Art critic. I:32

__ , Gwen. Earlier maid to Jane Marple. I:20:f

__ , Gwenda. Clerk in postoffice store. III:5

Hale, __ . Former police superintendent. I:24

Hale, Capt. "Bingo." Good friend of Merivale. III:2:f

Hall, Dr. __ . Operator of a nursing home. III:1

Hall, Archibald. Armed man in Basrah consulate general; English. XI:7

Halliday, __ . Young British scientist. I:5

Halliday, Mrs. __ . Wife of missing scientist. I:5

Hartington, Jack. An ardent golfer. I:28:f

Hartnell, Miss __ . Spinster in St. Mary Mead. I:29:c; II:1,3,9.

Harvey, Capt. __ . Member of British Intelligence Service. I:5

Harvey, Jim. Mechanic at Wychwood garage; engaged to Amy Gibbs. VI:3

Harwell, Capt. Richard. Daredevil horseman. I:40:g

Harwell, Mrs. Richard (Eleanor; nee Le Couteau). Wife of Richard H.; Canadian. I:40:g

Hassan. Egyptian expedition servant. I:3:f

Hastings, Mrs. __ . Woman with whom Miss Bartlett lived at St. Mary Mead. II:13

Hastings, Capt. Arthur. Friend, assistant, and sometime chronicler of Poirot. I:1-3,5,7-8,12,15; I:20:b; I:30:b-i; I:37:a,f; I:38:a; I:44

Hastings, Judith. Daughter of Capt. H.; assistant to Dr. Franklin. I:44

Hautet, M. __ . Juge d'instruction. I:2

Havering, Roger. Son of Baron Windsor. I:3:d

Havering, Mrs. Roger. Wife of Roger H. I:3:d

Hawes, __ . New curate. II:1

Hawker, Dr. __ . Physician; friend of Poirot. I:3:j

Hawker, Anthony. Boy friend of Mrs. Grace. I:26:i

Haworth, Maurice. Husband of Alistair H. XI:1:d

Haworth, Mrs. Maurice (Alistair). Dinner guest at the Lawes. XI:1:d

Hay, __ . Police sergeant. II:7

Haydock, Capt. __ . Retired naval officer. I:28:h

Haydock, Dr. __ . Physician in St. Mary Mead. I:29:d-e; II:1; II:2:m; II:3,9,14.

Haydock, Cmdr. __ . Retired naval officer; A.R.P. warden. III:3

Haydon, Elliot. Cousin of Sir Richard H.; impecunious barrister. II:2:b

Haydon, Sir Richard. Host at house party. II:2:b

Hayes, Supt. __ . Police official. I:4

Hayes, Sgt. __ . Village police sergeant. I:37:h

Hayling, Albert. Local constable. I:31

Haymes, Mrs. Phillipa (nee Pip Stamfordis). Widow of Ronald Haymes; lived with Miss Blacklock; assistant gardener at Dayas Hall. II:5

Hayward, Sir Arthur. Father of Charles H.; Asst. Comr. of Scotland Yard. XI:6

Hayward, Charles. In love with Sophie Leonides. XI:6

Hazy, Lady Selina. Friend of Jane Marple. II:11

Head, Mrs. __ . Gossiping cleaning woman for Miss Waterhouse. I:39

Hearn. __ . Detective inspector. I:26:j

III:2:i

Hope, Mildred. Part of quartet locked out of apartment. I:29:f

Hopkins, Nurse Jessie. District nurse; real name: Mary Riley Draper. I:22

Hopkinson, ___ . Legal adviser to Mrs. Harter. I:28:e

Horbury, Cicely, Countess of. Plane passenger. I:11

Horbury, Lord Stephen. Husband of Countess H. I:11

Horbury, Sydney. Nurse-attendant to Simeon Lee. I:19

Hori. Business manager to Imhotep. XI:5

Horlick, ___ . A gardener for Mrs. Welman. I:22

Horriston, Dr. ___ . Nursing home proprietor. III:2:g

Horrocks, Diana. Friend of Raymond West. II:10

Horsefall, Pamela. Newspaper writer. I:31

Horsefield, Sir Roderick. Uncle of Mrs. Restarick. I:41

Horsham, Henry. Foreign Office security official. XI:10

Horton, Maj. ___ . Bulldog fancier. VI:3

Hoskins, Robert. Local police constable. I:34

Howard, Evie (Evelyn). Companion of John Cavendish's stepmother. I:1

Howell, Mrs. ___ . Housekeeper at Chimneys. VI:2

Hubbard, Mrs. ___ . Sister of Felicity Lemon; student hostel matron. I:33

Hubbard, Mrs. Caroline Martha. Passenger on Orient Express; American. I:9

Hudd, Gina. Granddaughter of Carrie Louise Serrocold. II:6

Hudd, Walter ("Wally"). Husband of Gina; American. II:6

Huish, ___ . Police superintendent. IX:1

Humbleby, Dr. John W. Physician at Wychwood; deceased. VI:3

Humbleby, Mrs. John W. (Jessie Rose). Widow of Dr. H. VI:3

Humbleby, Rose. Daughter of the Humblebys. VI:3

Humphries, ___ . Manager of Bertram's Hotel. II:11

Hunt, Verity. Girl murdered in village that was on bus tour. II:13

Hunter, David. Brother of Mrs. Gordon Cloade; former commando. I:27

Hunter, Megan. Stepdaughter of Symmington. II:4

Hurst, Jim. Secretary to Caleb Blundell. IV:1:j

Hurstall, ___ . Butler at Gulls' Point. VI:4

Ibrahim. Expedition houseboy. I:13

Imhotep. A ka-priest and estate owner. XI:5

Ingles, John. Retired civil servant. I:5

Inglethorp, Alfred. Secretary to and second husband of Cavendish's stepmother. I:1

Inglethorp, Mrs. Emily Agnes (neé Cavendish). Stepmother of John Cavendish. I:1

Inglewood, Sir Mortimer. A K.C. I:26:f

Johnson, Miss ___ . Sister of organist. I:42
Johnson, ___ . Clerk in Robinson's firm. III:5
Johnson, ___ . New police constable at Market Basing. VI:1
Johnson, ___ . Leonides valet. XI:6
Johnson, Anne. Assistant on Leidner expedition. I:13
Johnson, Elspeth. Matron at Meadowbrook. I:35
Johnson, Mrs. Richard. "Relative" of Mrs. Lancaster. III:4
Johnson, Victoria. Hotel maid. II:10
Johnston, ___ . Millionaire; South African. I:37:f
Johnston, Elizabeth. Law student at hostel; West Indian. I:23
Johnstone, ___ . Police surgeon. II:8
Joliet, Mme. ___ . Operator of Ballet Maritski in Paris. II:8
Jonathan, Caleb. Retired lawyer. I:24
Jones, ___ . Traveling salesman for drug firm. II:2:a
Jones, Mrs. ___ . Wife of traveling salesman. II:2:a
Jones, ___ . Banker in Wychwood. VI:3
Jones, ___ . Detective sergeant. VI:4
Jones, Alice. Policewoman. I:34
Jones, Bobby. Son of Rev. Thomas J.; golfer. XI:2
Jones, Hetty. Daughter of bank manager. VI:3
Jones, Mrs. Mackenzie. Employer of Dorothy Pratt. XI:3:h
Jones, Mary. Daughter of inn landlord. I:40:g
Jones, Montgomery. Son of Lady Aileen Montgomery. I:38:1
Jones, Dr. Pauncefoot. Eminent archeologist. XI:7
Jones, Mrs. Pauncefoot. Wife of archeologist; real name: Anna
    Scheele. XI:7
Jones, Rev. Thomas. Vicar of Marchbolt. XI:2
Jones, Victoria. London typist; posed as: Venetia Savile. XI:7
Jones, William. Proprietor of Bells and Motley inn. I:40:g
Jordan, Mary. Formerly a cook in a village home. III:5
Jordan, Sinclair. Inamorata of Iris Wade. IV:1:d
Judd, Henry. Husband of Rosina Nunn. V:1:f

Kait. Wife of Sobek. XI:5
Kameni. A scribe. XI:5
Kane, ___ . Scotland Yard detective sergeant. I:29:a
Kane, Eva. Involved in former murder case; now missing; later
    name: Hope. I:31
Kane, Jonathan. Quasi-fascist leader of an earlier period. III:5
Kane, Norton. Bus companion of Poirot and Hastings. I:37:a
Keane, Marcia. Friend of Margery Gale. V:1:g
Keble, Ellen. Companion to Mrs. Samuelson. I:26:b
Keeley, David. Owner of Laidell house; brilliant mathematician.
    I:38:i
Keeley, Madge. Daughter of David K. I:38:i
Keene, Geoffrey. Secretary to Lytcham Roche. I:28:i

Keene, Ruby. Professional dancer; real name: Rosy Legge. II:3

Keene, Sylvia. Ward of Sir Ambrose Bercy. II:2:k

Kellett, Billy. A pickpocket. I:3:i

Kelsey, Inspector __ . Bexhill police officer. I:12, 35

Kelsey, Maj. __ . Employer of Nurse Leatheran. I:13

Kelsey, Mrs. Mary. Wife of Maj. K. I:13

Kelvin, __ . Landlord of Three Anchors tavern. II:2:c

Kemp, __ . Chief Inspector at New Scotland Yard. VII:2

Kendal, Tim. Manager of Golden Palm Hotel. II:10

Kendal, Mrs. Tim (Mollie). Wife of Tim K. II:10

Kennedy, Dr. James. Half-brother of Helen Kennedy Halliday. II:14

Kent, Capt. __ . In U.S. Secret Service. I:5

Kent, Charles. Murder suspect. I:4

Kent, Marcus. London doctor of Jerry Burton. II:4

Kenwood, __ . Air marshal. XI:10

Kerr, Dr. __ . Police surgeon at Andover. I:12

"Kerr, Mary." Name given to actress described by Jane Helier. II:2:l

Kerr, Hon. Venetia Anne. Plane passenger; daughter of Lord Cottesmore. I:11

Ketelly, Roderick. Young conspirator. XI:10

Kettering, Derek. Son-in-law of Van Aldin; heir to title of Lord Leconbury. I:6

Kettering, Mrs. Derek (Ruth). Daughter of Van Aldin. I:6

Khay. Husband of Renisenb; deceased. XI:5

Kidd, Kitty. Male impersonator. I:6

Kidder, Mrs. __ . Maid at Crackenthorpe house. II:8

Kidderminster, Lord __ . Father of Alexandra Farraday. VII:2

Kidderminster, Lady Victoria ("Vicky"). Mother of Alexandra Farraday. VII:2

Kiddle, Mrs. Bert. New occupant of the McGinty house. I:31

Kimble, Jim. Husband of Lily K. II:14

Kimble, Mrs. Jim (Lily; née Abbott). Formerly maid to the Hallidays. II:14

King, Beatrice. Formerly maid to Mrs. Oldfield. I:26:c

King, Donald. Medshot aerodrome manager. VII:1

King, Muriel. Former companion of Lady Esther Carr. IV:1:i

King, Sarah. Medical student. I:18

King, Winnie. Child who disappeared. I:26:j

Kingston Bruce, Beatrice. Daughter of Col. K.B. III:2:c

Kingston Bruce, Col. Charles. Retired officer. III:2:c

Kingston Bruce, Mrs. Charles. Wife of Col. K.B. III:2:c

Kirkwood, Frederick. Elderly lawyer for Trevelyan. X:1

Kleek, Sir James. Colleague of Lord Altamount. XI:10

Knight, Miss __ . Companion to Jane Marple. II:9

Knighton, Maj. Richard. Secretary to Van Aldin; alias: the Marquis. I:6

Kolinsky, Mrs. __ . Guest at Grand Hotel. I:35

Kramenin, __ . High-placed Russian agent. III:1

Kranin, __ . Interviewer of job applicants. XI:3:g

Lacey, Colin. Fifteen-year-old grandson of Col. Horace L. I:36:a

Lacey, Col. Horace. Owner of Kings Lacey manor. I:36:a

Lacey, Mrs. Horace (Emmeline). Wife of Col. L. L. I:36:a

Lacey, Sarah. Granddaughter of Col. L. I:36:a

Lacy, __ . Occupational therapist at Stonygates. II:6

Laidlaw, Maj. __ . Racing and gambling enthusiast. III:2:j

Laidlaw, Mrs. Marguerite. Wife of Maj. L.; French. III:2:j

Lake, Capt. __ . Estate agent for Chevenix-Gore. I:17:c

Lake, __ . Police sergeant. II:6

Lal, Chandra. Indian student at hostel. I:33

Lamb, Colin. Police sergeant; friend of Hardcastle; marine biologist. I:39; XI:6

Lambert, Mrs. Joyce. Applicant for job. XI:11:o

Lancaster, Mrs. __ . Patient at Sunny Ridge. III:4

Lancaster, Mrs. __ . House renter; widow. XI:1:e

Lancaster, Geoffrey. Son of Mrs. L. XI:1:e

Landor, James Stephen. Convicted of bank robbery. XI:4

Lane, Patricia. Archeology student living at hostel. I:33

Lane, Stephen. Clergyman staying at the Jolly Roger. I:23

Langdon, Miss __ . Proprietor of Golf Hotel. I:36:c

Langton, Claude. Offered to kill weeds for Harrison. I:37:b

Lanscombe, __ . Butler to recently deceased Richard Abernethie. I:32

Lansquenet, Mrs. Cora. Youngest sister of Richard Abernethie. I:32

Larkin, Mrs. Beryl. Party giver. I:26:i

Larraby, Dr. __ . Physician to Richard Abernethie. I:32

Last, __ . Police inspector. II:14

Latimer, Edward (Ted). Friend of Kay Strange. VI:4

Laurier, Henri. Man who assisted Hilary Craven in Fez; French. XI:8

Laverton-West, Charles. Fiancé of Mrs. Alden; an M.P. I:17:a

Lavigny, Father __ . Member of Leidner expedition; French; real name: Raoul Menier. I:13

Lavington, __ . A blackmailer. I:3:l

Lavington, "Dr." Ambrose. Medical specialist. I:28:f

Lawes, Rachel. Former fiancée of Macfarlane. XI:1:d

Lawson, Edgar. Stonygates resident; aide to Mr. Serrocold. II:6

Lawson, Wilhelmina (Minnie). Companion to Emily Arundell. I:15

Lawton, Mrs. __ . Aunt of Sheila Webb. I:39

Laxton, Harry. Caretaker. I:29:e

Laxton, Mrs. Harry (Louise). Wife of Harry L.; Anglo-French. I:29:e

Leith, Duchess of. Domineering peeress. V:1:f

Lejeune, __ . Divisional detective inspector. VIII:1

Le Marchant, __ . Una Drake's dinner date. I:38:l

Lemarchant, Caroline (Carla). Daughter of Amyas Crale. I:24

Lemarchant, Mrs. Louise. Aunt of Carla Crale L. I:24

Lemarchant, Simon. Uncle of Carla Crale L. I:24

Lementeuil, __ . Police official; Swiss. I:26:e

Lemesurier, Hugo. Uncle of Vincent L. I:30:e

Lemesurier, Mrs. Hugo (Sadie). Wife of Hugo L.; American. I:30:e

Lemesurier, Roger. Cousin of Vincent L. I:30:e

Lemesurier, Ronald. Eight-year-old elder son of Hugo L. I:30:e

Lemesurier, Capt. Vincent. Old friend of Hastings. I:30:e

Lemoine, M. __ . French Sûreté officer; originally: M. Chelles, *q.v.*
    VI:1

Lemon, Felicity. Secretary (at different times) to Poirot and Pyne.
    I:26:b,m; I:33-34; I:36:b; I:39,41

Lemprière, Joyce. Artist; once close friend of Raymond West. II:2:b-
    d,f.

__ , Leonard. Son of vicar at St. Mary Mead. II:8

Leonides, Aristide. Wealthy immigrant from Smyrna; Greek. XI:6

Leonides, Mrs. Aristide (Brenda). Young second wife of Aristide L.
    XI:6

Leonides, Eustace. Son of Philip L. XI:6

Leonides, Josephine. Daughter of Philip L. XI:6

Leonides, Philip. Younger son of Aristide L. XI:6

Leonides, Mrs. Philip (Magda). Wife of Philip L; actress; stage
    name: Magda West. XI:6

Leonides, Roger. Eldest son of Aristide L. XI:6

Leonides, Mrs. Roger (Clemency). Wife of Roger L.; scientist. XI:6

Leonides, Sophia Katherine. Daughter of Philip L.; Foreign Office
    official in Egypt. XI:6

__ , Leonie. Maid to Mrs. Vanderlyn; French. I:17:b

__ , Leonie. Maid to Mrs. Conrad; French. I:30:h

__ , Leonie. Childhood nurse to Gwenda Reed. II:14

Lessing, Ruth. Secretary to George Barton. VII:2

Lester, Charles. Bank clerk. I:3:m

Lestrange, Mrs. Estelle. Recent resident at St. Mary Mead. II:1

Letardeau, Raoul. Fourth man in train compartment. I:28:c

Leverson, Charles. Nephew of Sir Reuben Astwell. I:36:c

Lewes, __ . Maid to the Christows. I:25

Lewis, __ . Lawyer. VI:4

Li Chang Yen. A Mandarin allegedly aiming at disintegration of
    civilization. I:5

__ , Lily. Fiancée of Harry. II:9

Linch, Gladys. Maid to Mrs. Jones. II:2:a

Lindstrom, Kirsten. Maid to the Argyles. IX:1

Lingard, Miss __ . Writer assisting Chevenix-Gore. I:17:c

I:26:e

Luxton, Mrs. __ . Elderly village lady. III:5

Lyall, Pamela. Vacationer at Rhodes. I:17:d

Lyndon, Miss __ . Secretary to Strange. I:10

Lyon, Mrs. Maureen. Tenant in Culver Street house; real name: Gregg. I:29:a

Lytcham Roche, Hubert. Owner of Lytcham Close. I:28:i

Lytcham Roche, Mrs. __ . Wife of Hubert L.R. I:28:i

Lytton Gore, Hermione ("Egg"). Daughter of Lady L.G. I:10

Lytton Gore, Lady Mary. Impoverished widow. I:10

Maberly, Diana. Girl with broken engagement. I:26:h

MacAdam, David. British Prime Minster. I:3:h

Macalister, Miss __ . Nursery governess of Despard children; Scottish. VIII:1

MacAllister, Dr. __ . Uncle of Comdr. Challenger; gynecologist. I:7

MacAndrew, Dr. __ . Physician; Scottish. I:36:d

Macarthur, Gen. John Gordon. World War I officer. XI:4

Macatta, Mrs. __ . An M.P.; authority on housing. I:17:b; VI:2

MacDonald, __ . Head gardener at Chimneys; Scottish. VI:2

MacDougal, Dr. __ . Physician in Loomouth. I:10

Mace, Albert. Chemist's shop pharmacist. I:1

Macfarlane, __ . Friend of Dickie Carpenter; Scottish. XI:1:d

MacKenzie, Mrs. Helen. Sanatorium patient. II:7

Mackenzie, Janet. Maid to Miss French. I:28:a

MacMaster, Dr. __ . Retired physician who had treated the Argyles. IX:1

MacNaughton, Miss __ . Nurse to Lady Grayle. IV:1:k

MacQueen, Hector Willard. Secretary to Ratchett. I:9

MacWhirter, Andrew. A down-and-outer; made unsuccessful suicide attempt. VI:4

"Maddie." *See* Mlle. Rouselle. I:43

__ , Madeleine. Maid to Countess of Horbury; actually: daughter of Mme. Giselle. I:11

Mahmoud. Dragoman on Petra trip. I:18

Maine, __ . Scotland Yard inspector. XI:4

Maitland, Capt. __ . Police official. I:13

Malinowski, Ladislaus. Racing driver; half French, half Polish. II:11

Mallaby, Mrs. __ . Widow; American. I:30:c

Maltravers, __ . A recent possible suicide. I:3:b

Maltravers, Mrs. __ . Widow of recently deceased. I:3:b

Manders, Oliver. Neighbor and dinner guest of Cartwright. I:10

Manelli, Giuseppe. Waiter and spy in London hotel. VI:1

Manly, __ . Scheduled to play Pierrot in a masquerade. V:1:1

Mannering, Lady __ . Guest at Silent Garden house party. II:2:b

Mannering, Violet. Daughter of Lady M. II:2:b

Manning, __ . Inglethorp gardener. I:1
Manning, __ . Protheroe chauffeur. II:1
Manning, __ . Replacement gardener for the Reeds. II:14
Mansur. Expedition houseboy. I:13
__ , Manuel. Gardener at mountaintop villa; Spanish. V:1:k
Marbury, Mrs. __ . Landlady to Cust. I:12
Marbury, Lily. Girl living in Cust's rooming house. I:12
March, Cicely. Young lady answering newspaper ad. III:2:p
Marchand, __ . *Sergent de ville* in Merlinville. I:2
Marchand, Mlle. Felise. Girl in garden adjoining golf course. I:28:f
Marchington, Lord __ . Father of Frankie Derwent. XI:2
Marchmont, Mrs. Adela. Widowed sister of Gordon Cloade. I:27
Marchmont, Lynn. Daughter of Mrs. Adela M. I:27
Margrave, Lily. Companion to Lady Astwell; real name: Naylor.
   I:36:c
__ , Maria. Cook at hostel; wife of Geronimo. I:33
__ , Maria. Maid to Ariadne Oliver. I:43
__ , Marie. Former maid to Linnet Ridgeway. I:16
Marie Angelique. Nun; Belgian. XI:1:a
__ , Marjorie. Abernethie cook. I:32
Marks, Miss __ . Secretary to Pengelly. I:30:f
Marle, Hector. Father of Iris M.; deceased. VII:2
Marle, Iris. Daughter of Hector M. VII:2
"the Marquis." Master criminal. I:6
Marrascaud, __ . Notorious criminal; alias: Robert. I:26:e
Marriot, __ . Scotland Yard detective inspector. III:2:c
Marroway, Sir George. Yachting party guest of Pointz. I:20:a
Marroway, Lady Pamela. Yachting party guest of Pointz. I:20:a
Marsden, __ . A Scotland Yard chief inspector. I:22
Marsdon, Tony (Anthony). Friend of Deborah Beresford; a coder.
   III:3
Marsh, Andrew. Uncle of Violet M. I:3:k
Marsh, Geraldine. Daughter of Lord Edgware. I:8
Marsh, Capt. Ronald. Nephew of Lord Edgware. I:8
Marsh, Violet. Client of Poirot. I:3:k
Marshall, Capt. __ . Estate agent. I:28:i
Marshall, Andrew. Lawyer for Argyle family. IX:1
Marshall, Mrs. Arlena Stuart. Guest at Jolly Roger; former actress.
   I:23
Marshall, Capt. Kenneth. Husband of Arlena. I:23
Marshall, Linda. Daughter of Capt. M. I:23
Marston, Anthony James. Driver of powerful car. XI:4
__ , Martha. Maid at San Souci hotel. III:3
__ , Martha. Crabtree maid. XI:3:d
Martin, Miss __ . Stenographer to Ryland. I:5
Martin, Mrs. Alix (née King). Recently married; former typist.
   I:28:g

Martin, Bryan. Film actor; companion of Jane Wilkinson. I:8
Martin, Elizabeth. Girl at Monte Carlo party; American. V:1:e
Martin, Gerald. Husband of Alix M. I:28:g
Martin, Gladys. Fortescue parlormaid. II:7
Martindale, __ . A solicitor. VI:4
Martindale, Katherine ("Sandy Cat"). President of a typing
    bureau. I:39
__ , Martine. Supposed friend or wife of Edmund Crackenthorpe,
    killed in the War. II:8
Marvel, Sir Donald. An M.P. IV:1:j
Marvell, __ . Solicitor for James Reilly. III:2:i
Marvell, Mary. Film star. I:3:a
__ , Mary. Cook-maid at vicarage. II:1
__ , Mary. Housemaid in a rooming house. II:2:j
__ , Mary. Maid to Mrs. Bantry. II:3
__ , Mary. Aunt of Joyce Lambert. XI:11:o
Mary Ursula, Sister. A nun; Irish; earlier name: Kate Casey. I:26:l
Mason, Ada Beatrice. Maid to Ruth Kettering; real name: Kitty
    Kidd. I:6
Mason, Jane. Maid to Mrs. Carrington; real name: Gracie Kidd.
    I:30:f
Massington, Mrs. __ . Friend of Iris Wade. IV:1:d
Masterman, Edward Henry. Valet to Ratchett. I:9
Masters, __ . Chauffeur to Renauld. I:2
Masters, __ . Chauffeur to Satterthwaite. I:38:h; I:40:g
Masters, Charlie. Farm laborer. I:31
Masterton, Jim. Fiancé of Barbara St. Vincent. XI:3:a
Masterton, Wilfrid. An M.P. I:34
Masterton, Mrs. Wilfrid. Wife of M.P. I:34
Matcham, Mrs. __ . Old nanny of friends of Ravenscrofts. I:43
__ , Mathew. Great-great-uncle of Stroud and Rossiter. I:29:b
Mathias, John. Gardener for Capt. Harwell. I:40:g
__ , Maud. Fiancée of Edward Robinson. XI:3:e
Maverick, Dr. __ . Psychiatrist at Stonygates. II:6
Maxwell, __ . Police superintendent at Exeter. X:1
Mayerling, __ . Secret Service man. I:5
Mayfield, Lord (Sir Charles McLaughlin). Engineer; Minister of
    Armaments. I:17:b
Mayherne, __ . Lawyer. I:28:a
Mayhew, __ . Solicitor representing Charles Leverson. I:36:c
Mayhew, George. Solicitor. I:24
McClelland, Sister __ . Nurse to Mrs. Goedler. II:5
McCrae, Mrs. __ . Canon Pennyfather's housekeeper. II:11
McCulloch, Dr. __ . Physician to Prof. Shoreham. XI:10
McGillicuddy, Mrs. Elspeth. Train passenger. II:8
McGinty, Mrs. __ . Murdered charwoman; widow. I:31
McGrath, Jimmy. Old friend of Anthony Cade. VI:1

Metcalf, Dr. __ . Physician in Danemouth. II:3
Meynell, Dr. __ . Physician to Mrs. Harter. I:28:e
__ , Michael. Repertory actor. I:31
__ , Michael. Young friend of Colin Lacey. I:36:a
Michaelovna, Anna. Colleague of Count Streptitch; actually:
    Princess Poporensky. XI:3:g
Michel, Pierre. Train conductor. I:6
Michel, Pierre. Conductor on Orient Express. I:9
"Middleton, Mrs. __ ." Housekeeper to Haverings. I:3:d
Middleton, Mrs. Diana. A widow. I:36:a
Miles, __ . Butler to Dwighton. I:29:i
Miller, Inspector __ . C.I.D. official. I:36:b-c
__ , Milly. Wife of Albert Batt. III:4
__ , Milly. Maid to Ariadne Oliver. VIII:1
Milray, Violet. Secretary and household supervisor for Cartwright.
    I:10
Minton, Sophia. Resident at San Souci hotel. III:3
Mirabelle. Parisian stage favorite. V:1:e
__ , Mirelle. A dancer. I:6
Mitchell, Henry. Senior plane steward. I:11
Mitchell, Maj. Robert. Chief constable of police. VI:4
__ , Mitzi. Cook at Blacklocks. II:5
Mohammed. Dragoman on Nile trip. IV:1:k
__ , Molly. Waitress in Galant Endeavor restaurant. I:36:d
Monckton, Col. __ . Dinner guest of Satterthwaite. V:1:i
Moncrieffe, Jean. Dispenser for Dr. Oldfield. I:26:c
Monro, Flossie. Woman contacted through Poirot's solicitor. I:5
Montresor, Mary. Society girl. XI:3:j
Montressor, Helen. "Second cousin" of Alistair Blunt; real name:
    Gerda Grant. I:21
Montu. Egyptian embalmer. XI:5
Moody, Mrs. Elizabeth. Patient at Sunny Ridge. III:4
Mooney, Kitty. Young shipboard passenger. I:20:i
Morales, Pedro. Diner at adjoining table to Barton party. VII:2
Morecombe, Lady Edwina. Godmother of Sarah Lacey. I:36:a
Morganthal, Otto. Employer of Anna Scheele; international
    banker. XI:7
Morley, Georgina. Sister of dentist. I:21
Morley, Henry. Dentist. I:21
Morris, Dr. __ . Physician in Annesley case. I:38:i
Morris, Dr. __ . Retired physician; practice taken over by Quimper.
    II:8
Morris, Isaac. Go-between to Capt. Lombard. XI:4
Morton, __ . Police inspector. I:32
Mosgorovsky, __ . Operator of Seven Dials Club; Russian. VI:2
Moss, Edwin. Theatrical agent. I:37:h
Moss, Mary ("Zobeida"). Former dancer; sister of Edwin M.;

Nunn, Rosina. Actress. V:1:f
Nye, Pamela. Sister of Sir Stafford N.; deceased. XI:10
Nye, Sir Stafford. Foreign Office official. XI:10

Obolovitch, Prince Michael. British candidate for the
    Herzoslovakian throne; *see* Count Stanislaus. VI:1
O'Brien, Nurse __. Attendant on Mrs. Welman. I:22
O'Connor, Sgt. __. Scotland Yard police sergeant. I:14
O'Connor, Derek. Foreign Office official. I:35
Ogilvie, Alexander. Agent for George Barton in Buenos Aires. VII:2
Oglander, Miss __. Daughter of John O. I:30:g
Oglander, Mrs. __. Diner at Savoy at table next to Una Drake. I:38:1
Oglander, John. Owner of country estate. I:30:g
Oglander, Mrs. John. Wife of estate owner. I:30:g
Oglander, John, Jr. Son of John O. I:30:g
O'Hara, Eileen. Lady who fainted on shipboard. III:2:p
Ohlsson, Greta. Nurse; matron in missionary school; Swedish. I:9
O'Keefe, __. Nurse at Sunny Ridge. III:4
Olafsson, Eric. Industrialist; Swedish. XI:10
Olde, Sir Malcolm. A K.C. retained to defend Rhodes. I:20:f
Oldfield, Dr. Charles. Country physician. I:26:c
Olga, Grand Duchess. Woman who gave jewels to Roberts on train.
    IV:1:e
Oliver, Mrs. Ariadne. Prolific detective story writer; feminist;
    friend of Poirot. I:14,31,34,41-43; IV:1:b; VIII:1
Olivera, Jane. Grandniece of Alistair Blunt. I:21
Olivera, Mrs. Julia. Mother of Jane O. I:21
Olivier, Mme. __. Famous scientist; French. I:5
O'Murphy, __. Prime Minister's chauffeur. I:3:h
"O'Neill, Dr. __." Member of Society for Physical Research. III:2:n
Opalsen, Mrs. __. Stockbroker's wife. I:3:g
Opalsen, Ed. Rich stockbroker. I:3:g
Oranoff, Prince Sergius Ivanovitch. Dance enthusiast; Russian.
    V:1:l
O'Rourke, Mrs. __. Resident at San Souci hotel. III:3
O'Rourke, Flight Lt. __. Young officer at Damascus. IV:1:b
O'Rourke, Terence. Air Minister. VI:2
Osborne, Zachariah. Proprietor of a chemist's shop. VIII:1
Oscar, Miss __. Stenographer to Lomax. VI:1
Ossington, Sir William ("Billy Bones"). Assistant Commissioner at
    Scotland Yard. VI:3
Otterbourne, Rosalie. Daughter of Mrs. O. I:16
Otterbourne, Mrs. Salome. Tourist on Nile trip; novelist. I:16
Oulard, Denise. Servant of Renauld; French. I:2
Oulard, Léonie. Renauld maid. I:2
"Owen, Ulrich Norman." Owner of Indian Island. XI:4
Oxley, Mrs. Lou (Louisa). Niece of Joan West. I:36:f

Paaopolous, Aristide. Head waiter in night club; Greek. I:26:m
Pace, Harrington. Uncle of Roger Havering. I:3:d
Packard, Millicent. Superintendent of Sunny Ridge rest home. III:4
Packer, Mrs. __ . Woman given to premonitions. I:39
Packham, Sir George. Cabinet undersecretary. XI:10
Packington, George. Husband of Mrs. Maria P. IV:1:a
Packington, Mrs. George (Maria). Client of Parker Pyne. IV:1:a
Pagett, Edith. Former cook for the Hallidays. II:14
Pagett, Guy. Secretary to Sir Eustace Pedler. VII:1
Palgrave, Maj. __ . Retired officer with glass eye. II:10
Palgrove, Edward. Fiancé of Dorothy Pratt. XI:3:h
Palk, __ . Police constable. I:29:c; II:3
Palliser, Sir Edward. A K.C.; former criminal barrister. XI:3:d
Palmer, Mabel. Nurse to Mr. Templeton. I:5
Papopolous, Demetrius. Dealer in antiques. I:6
Papopolous, Zia. Daughter of Demetrius P. I:6
Paravicini, __ . Guest at Monkswell Manor. III:4
Pardoe, William Reuben. Cousin of Ellie Rogers. XI:9
"Pardonstenger, Mrs. __ ." Occupant of country house; real name:
    Mrs. Rube Wallace. XI:3:j
Parfitt, Canon __ . Clergyman. I:28:c
Parker, __ . Ackroyd butler. I:4
Parker, __ . Guest of Walter Protheroe. I:30:d
Parker, Mrs. __ . Guest of Walter Protheroe. I:30:d
Parker, Bernard. Guest of Hardman. I:37:f
Parker, Gerald. Friend of Hastings. I:3:c
Parkins, Sgt. __ . Police sergeant at Lymstock. II:4
Parkinson, Alexander Richard. Marker of a message in an old
    book; deceased. III:5
Parminter, __ . Scotland Yard inspector. I:29:a
Parrott, James. Law partner of Entwhistle. I:32
Parsons, __ . Butler to Sir Reuben Astwell. I:36:c
Parsons, Olive. Student in Sylvia Battle's school. VI:4
Partridge, __ . Maid to Joanna Burton. II:4
Partridge, James. Bank clerk. I:12
Paterson, __ . A carter. I:30:i
Paton, Capt. Ralph. Stepson of Roger Ackroyd. I:4
Patterson, Mrs. Elsie. Sister of Gerda Christow. I:25
Patterson, Phyllis. Fiancée of Arthur Carmichael. XI:1:i
Paul, Prince. Prince of Maurania; alias: Count Feodor. I:30:g
Pauline, Grand Duchess. Double of Jane Cleveland. XI:3:g
Paulovitch, Count Sergius. Member of criminal ring. VII:1
Pavett, __ . Valet to Derek Kettering. I:6
Pavlovitch, Count Alexis. Restaurant proprietor. I:26:d
Paynter, __ . Rich globetrotter; killed at Market Handford. I:5
Paynter, Gerald. Artist; nephew of man killed. I:5
Peabody, Caroline. Friend of Emily Arundell. I:15

Pearson, __ . Mining company director. I:3:m
Pearson, Mrs. __ . Poirot's landlady. I:5
Pearson, Brian. Nephew of Trevelyan. X:1
Pearson, James. Nephew of Trevelyan; insurance office employee. X:1
Pebmarsh, __ . A coroner. I:27
Pebmarsh, Millicent. A blind Braille teacher. I:39
Pedler, Sir Eustace. Owner of Mill House; an M.P. VII:1
Pender, Dr. __ . Clergyman in St. Mary Mead. II:2:b-c,e
Penderley, __ . Head of a Dillmouth real estate firm. II:14
Pengelly, Edward. Dentist. I:30:f
Pengelly, Mrs. Edward. Wife of dentist. I:30:f
Penn, Elizabeth. Owner of antique shop. I:37:a
Penn, Sir Josiah. Retired major general. III:4
Pennington, Andrew. Lawyer; trustee for Linnet Ridgeway; American. I:16
Pennyfather, Canon __ . Elderly clergyman. II:11
Pennyman, Maj. __ . Englishman in Baghdad. I:13
Penrose, Dr. __ . Head of Saltmarsh sanatorium. II:14
Pentemian, Mrs. __ . Mother traveling with son to Baghdad; American. IV:1:h
Percehouse, Caroline. Elderly renter of a Trevelyan cottage; spinster. X:1
Perenna, Mrs. Eileen. Proprietress of San Souci hotel in Leahampton. III:3
Perenna, Sheila. Daughter of Mrs. Eileen P. III:3
Perrot, Jules. Airline clerk; French. I:11
Perry, Amos. Husband of the "Friendly Witch." III:4
Perry, Mrs. Amos (Alice). The "Friendly Witch" in a long imagined house. III:4
Perry, Percy. Editor of a scandal paper. I:26:f
Peters, Andrew. Research chemist; American. XI:8
Peters, Willard. Son of Mrs. Willard P. IV:1:l
Peters, Mrs. Willard J. Guest in a Greek luxury hotel; widow. IV:1:l
Petherick, __ . Jane Marple's solicitor. I:20:f; II:2:e
Pettigrew, __ . A secretary to Sir Eustace Pedler in Africa. VII:1
Peverell, __ . Elderly butler to the Laceys. I:36:a
Phelps, Hayward. London journalist; friend of Battle; American. VI:2
Philips, __ . A K.C. I:1
Phillpot, Maj. __ . Owner of Gipsy's Acre. X:9
Pierce, __ . Young police constable. I:39
Pierce, Mrs. __ . Elderly cleaning woman for Mrs. Allen. I:17:a
Pierce, Mrs. __ . Proprietor of a cigaret shop. VI:3
Pierce, Anabel. Passenger to Petra. I:18
Pierce, Tommy. Choir boy; son of cigaret shop proprietor. VI:3
Pikeaway, Col. Ephraim. Secret agent. I:35; III:5; XI:10

Plenderleith, Jane. Friend and roommate of Mrs. Allen. I:17:a
Pleydon, Gene. Young man over whom two girls fought. VIII:1
Pointz, Isaac. Diamond merchant. I:20:a
Poirot, Achille. "Twin brother" of Hercule P. I:5
Poissonier, M. __ . Member of French government. XI:10
Poli, Gen. __ . Retired officer on Damascus-Baghdad trip; Italian. IV:1:h
Politt, Miss __ . Seamstress. I:29:c
Pollard, __ . Police constable. I:30:d
Pollock, __ . Police sergeant at Exhampton. X:1
Pollock, Alfred. Gardener for Miss Greenshaw. I:36:f
Polonska, Vanda. Foreign refugee near Leahampton; Polish. III:3
Pope, Lavinia. Proprietress of girls' school in Paris. I:26:j
Portal, Alec. Avid sportsman. V:1:a
Portal, Mrs. Alec (Eleanor). Wife of Alec P.; Australian. V:1:a
Porter, Maj. George Douglas. Retired Indian army officer. I:27
Porter, Maj. John. Big-game hunter. V:1:b
Potter, Mike. Small boy who summoned priest. VIII:1
Power, Emery. Financier; art collector. I:26:1
Pratt, Dorothy. Parlormaid to Mrs. Mackenzie Jones. XI:3:h
Prescott, __ . Manager of Majestic Hotel. II:3
Prescott, __ . Cook for Pye. II:4
Prescott, Canon Jeremy. Clergyman. II:10
Prescott, Joan. Sister of Canon P. II:10
Preston, Hailey. Aide to Marina Gregg. II:9
Price, Emlyn. Young tour passenger. II:13
Price Ridley, Mrs. __ . Prosperous widow in St. Mary Mead. I:29:e; II:1,3; III:5
Primer, __ . Detective inspector. II:14
Pritchard, Alex. Man who fell over cliff; real name: Alan Carstairs. XI:2
Pritchard, George. A widower. I:38:f
Pritchard, Mrs. George (Mary). Hypochondriac former wife of George P. I:38:f
Protheroe, Lettice. Daughter of Col. Lucius P. II:1
Protheroe, Col. Lucius. Church warden. II:1
Protheroe, Mrs. Lucius (Anne). Second wife of Col. P. II:1
Protheroe, Walter. Resident of Market Basing; deceased; real name: Wendover. I:30:d
Pryce, Miss __ . Aunt of Netta P. IV:1:h
Pryce, Netta. Young tourist on Damascus-Baghdad trip. IV:1:h
Pugh, Eric. Friend of Nye. XI:10
Purdy, Prof. __ . Archeologist. I:39
Purvis, William. Solicitor to Emily Arundell. I:15
Pye, __ . Rich occupant of Prior's End at Lymstock. II:4

Quant, Esther. Parlormaid to Lois Hargreaves. III:2:1

Quentin, Dr. __ . Physician attending Paynter. I:5
Quentin, __ . Butler to St. Vincent. XI:3:a
Quimper, Dr. __ . Family doctor. II:8

Radclyffe, Capt. Dennis. Nephew of Lady Radclyffe's husband.
 III:2:l
Radclyffe, Lucy. Wealthy aunt of Lois Hargreaves. III:2:l
Raddish, __ . House agent. XI:1:e
Radley, Gen. __ . Frequent guest at Bertram's Hotel. II:11
Radnor, Jacob. A tailor. I:30:f
Radzky, Countess __ . Wealthy widow; Hungarian. VI:2
Rafiel, Jason. Rich supermarket chain owner; vacationing in
 Caribbean. II:10
Rafiel, Michael. Imprisoned son of Jason R. II:13
Raglan, __ . Police inspector. I:4,42; VI:2
Raikes, Mrs. __ . Farmer's wife. I:1
Raikes, Howard. Dental patient. I:21
Ram, Gopal. Student at hostel; Indian. I:33
Ramona, Dolores. Aide to Pyne; alias: Madeleine de Sara; real
 name; Maggie Sayers. I:20:d
Ramsay, Mrs. __ . Near neighbor of Miss Pebmarsh. I:39
Ramsay, Bill. Son of Mrs. R. I:39
Ramsay, Ted. Younger son of Mrs. R. I:39
Ramsbottom, Effie. Sister-in-law of Fortescue. II:7
Ransom, Nicholas. Youth at party. I:42
Ratchett, Samuel Edward. Passenger on Orient Express; real
 name: Cassetti. I:9
Rathbone, Dr. __ . Employer of Edward Goring. XI:7
Rathbone, Denis. Beau of Ann Shapland. I:35
Rattery, John. Fiancé of Carla Crale. I:24
Ravel, Annette. An orphan; French. I:28:c
Ravenscroft, Celia. Daughter of Sir Alistair R.; goddaughter of
 Ariadne Oliver. I:43
Ravenscroft, Edward. Younger brother of Celia R. I:43
Rawlinson, Dr. __ . Local physician. II:2:f
Rawlinson, Bob. Pilot for and good friend of Ali. I:35
"Rayburn, Harry." "Secretary" to Sir Eustace Pedler; alias: Parker,
 VII:1
Raymond, Geoffrey. Secretary to Ackroyd. I:4
Read, Vera. Secretary to Mme. Nazorkoff. XI:3:l
Redcliffe, Hermia. Friend of Easterbrook. VIII:1
Redding, Lawrence. Young artist. II:1
Redfern, Mrs. Christine. Guest at the Jolly Roger. I:23
Redfern, Patrick. Husband of Mrs. Christine R. I:23
Reece-Holland, Claudia. Roommate of Norma Restarick; daughter
 of Emlyn R.-H.; a secretary. I:41
Reece-Holland, Emlyn. An M.P. I:41

Reed, Giles. Buyer of house in southern England. II:14
Reed, Mrs. Giles (Gwenda). Wife of Giles R.; New Zealander. II:14
Reedburn, Henry. An impresario; neighbor of the Oglanders. I:30:g
Rees-Talbot, Mary. Old friend of Col. Race; employer of Betty
    Archdale. VII:2
Reeves, __ . Police inspector. I:28:i
Reeves, __ . Butler to Protheroe. II:1
Reeves, __ . Ship passenger to Africa; member of South African
    Labor party. VII:1
Reeves, Pamela. Missing Girl Guide. II:3
Reichardt, Dr. __ . Psychologist; German. XI:10
Reid, __ . Purported lawyer from Melbourne. IV:1:b
Reilly, __ . Dentist; partner of Henry Morley. I:21
Reilly, Dr. Giles. Physician. I:13
Reilly, James. Author of *Pacifist Poems*. III:2:i
Reilly, Sheila. Daughter of Dr. Giles R. I:13
Reiter, Carl. Photographer with Leidner expedition; American. I:13
Renauld, Jack. Son of the Renaulds. I:2
Renauld, Paul. Applicant for Poirot's services; real name: Georges
    Conneau; French-Canadian. I:2
Renauld, Mme. Paul (Eloise). Widow of Paul R. I:2
Rendell, Dr. __ . Former employer of Mrs. McGinty. I:31
Rendall, Fred. Boy friend of Agnes Woddell. II:4
Rendell, Mrs. Shelagh. Wife of Dr. R. I:31
Renisenb. Daughter of Imhotep; widow of Khay. XI:5
Rennie, __ . Visitor to the Kingston Bruces. III:2:c
Restarick, Alex. Brother of Stephen R. II:6
Restarick, Andrew. Nephew by marriage of Sir Roderick
    Horsefield; real name: Robert Orwell. I:41
Restarick, Mrs. Andrew (Mary). Stepmother of Norma R.; alias:
    Frances Cary. I:41
Restarick, Mrs. Grace. First wife of Andrew R.; deceased. I:41
Restarick, Norma. Girl referred to Poirot by Ariadne Oliver. I:41
Restarick, Simon. Older brother of Andrew R.; deceased. I:41
Restarick, Stephen. Stepson of Carrie Louise Serrocold. II:6
Revel, Mrs. Virginia (neé Cawthron). Widow; daughter of Lord
    Edgbarton; cousin of Lomax. VI:1
Reynolds, Mrs. __ . Mother of Joyce R. I:42
Reynolds, Ann. Guest at party; sister of Joyce R. I:42
Reynolds, Joyce. Guest at party. I:42
Reynolds, Leopold. Brother of Joyce R. I:42
Rhodes, __ . Man who called, with Petherick, on Jane Marple. I:20:f
Rhodes, Mrs. Amy. Hypochondriac wife of Petherick's
    companion; deceased. I:20:f
Rice, Mrs. __ . Mother of Mrs. Clayton. I:26:g
Rice, __ . Police inspector. I:29:a
Rice, Dicky. Friend of le Marchant; saw Una Drake at Torquay.

I:38:1

Rice, Mrs. Frederica. Friend of Nick Buckley. I:7

Rice, Thomas. Oriental counselor in British embassy at Baghdad. XI:7

Rich, Maj. Charles. Well-to-do bachelor. I:36:b

Rich, Eileen. Geography and English teacher. I:35

Richards, __ . Valet to U.S. ambassador. III:2:p

Richards, Mrs. Anne. Daughter of Mme. Giselle. I:11

Richetti, Guido. Archeologist. I:16

Richmond, Alfred. Chief county police constable. I:42

Richmond, Arthur. Officer under Gen. Macarthur; killed in action. XI:4

Riddell, Albert. Customer of Mrs. Ascher. I:12

Riddle, Maj. __ . Chief constable; old friend of Poirot. I:17:c

Rider, Miss __ . Housekeeper to Dr. Hawkins. I:3:j

Ridge, Samuel. Orchestra conductor. XI:3:1

Ridgeway, Dr. __ . Neighbor of Poirot. I:5

Ridgeway, Charles. Nephew of Mrs. Harter. I:28:e

Ridgeway, Linnet. Wealthy girl; orphan. I:16

Ridgeway, Philip. Bank employee; nephew of Vavasour. I:3:e

Rieger, Katrina. Nurse to Miss Barrowby. I:20:c

Rigg, Dr. __ . Police surgeon. I:39

Riseley-Porter, Mrs. Geraldine. Tour passenger. II:13

Rival, Mrs. Merlina. Murdered man was possibly her long-missing husband; real name: Flossie Gapp. I:39

Rivers, __ . Chauffeur whom Easterfield discharged. VI:3

Rivington, Mrs. Hubert. Wife of couple who had escorted Carstairs. XI:2

Robbins, Edward. Man who saw Betty Sprot. III:3

__ , Robert. Dismissed waiter at Swiss mountain resort. I:26:e

__ , Robert. London picture gallery proprietor; old friend of Tommy. III:4

Roberts, Dr. __ . Coroner at Much Benham. II:1

Roberts, __ . Taxi driver in St. Mary Mead. II:9

Roberts, __ . Client of Pyne; sought for excitement. IV:1:e

Roberts, Mrs. __ . Housekeeper for Vicar Jones. XI:2

Roberts, Dr. Geoffrey. Physician consulted by Battle about murder. I:14

Robertson, Dr. __ . West Indian police doctor. II:10

Robertson, __ . Man offering to help Col. Pikeaway. I:35

Robinson, __ . Consulted by Davy about ownership of Bertram's Hotel. II:11

Robinson, __. Man interviewed by Tommy, perhaps in Intelligence. III:5

Robinson, __ . Financier. XI:10

Robinson, Edward. A clerk. XI:3:e

Robinson, John. Acquaintance of Gerald Parker. I:3:c

Rowland, William. Uncle and former employee of George R. XI:3:c

Rowlandson, ___ . Manager of Royal Spa Hotel. II:5

Rowley, Mrs. ___ . Landlady of Deborah Beresford. III:3

Royde, Thomas. Operator of a Malay plantation; distant cousin of Audrey Strange. VI:4

Rubec, Dr. ___ . Psychologist at leper hospital; Swiss. XI:8

Rudd, Jason ("Jinks"). Film director; husband of Marina Gregg. II:9

Rudge, Franklin. Smitten by Countess Czarnova; American. V:1:e

Runcorn, Lady ___ . Guest of Hardman; a *grande dame*. I:37:f

Rundle, Bert. Constable at Lymstock. II:4

Russell, Miss ___ . Ackroyd housekeeper. I:4

Russell, Barton. Wealthy businessman; American. I:20:e

Rustington, Mrs. Janet. Yachting party guest of Pointz. I:20:a

Rustonbury, Lady ___ . Patron of the arts. XI:3:l

Ryan, Dr. ___ . Physician. I:30:g

Ryan, William P. Newspaper correspondent; American. XI:1:a

Rycroft, ___ . Elderly book lover and bird enthusiast; criminologist. X:1

Rycroft, Sir Lewis. Former lover of Mrs. Welman; deceased. I:22

Ryder, Hank. Wealthy man; American. III:2:j

Ryder, James Bell. Plane passenger; cement company manager. I:11

Rydesdale, George. Chief constable of Middleshire. II:5

Ryland, Abe. Incredibly rich soap king; American. I:5

Rymer, Mrs. Abner (Amelia). Client of Parker Pyne; later called: Hannah Moorhouse. IV:1:f

Sainsbury Seale, Mabelle. Dental patient. I:21

Saintclair, Valerie. A dancer. I:30:g

St. John, Gerald. Considerably older than wife. I:40:h

St. John, Mrs. Gerald (Daphne). Girl who stole diamond ring; real name: Ernestine Richards. I:40:h

St. John, Jewel ("Jill"). Young daughter of Walter S.J. I:37:h

St. John, Walter Edmund. Man shot in village. I:37:h

St. Vincent, Mrs. ___ . Indigent widow. XI:3:a

St. Vincent, Barbara. Daughter of Mrs. S.V. XI:3:a

St. Vincent, Lawrence. Nephew and heir of the Earl of Cheriton. III:2:b

St. Vincent, Rupert. Son of Mrs. S.V. XI:3:a

Samoushenka, Katrina. Ballet dancer; Russian. I:26:d

Samuelson, Mrs. ___ . Owner of kidnapped dog. I:26:b

Sandbourne, Mrs. ___ . Tour director. II:13

Sandbourne, William. Man who died in church; real name: Walter St. John. I:37:h

Sandeman, Sir Edwin. Harley Street doctor called to see Fortescue. II:7

Shaitana, __ . Rich host at bridge party. I:14
Shane, Michael. Actor; husband of Rosamund S. I:32
Shane, Mrs. Michael (Rosamund). Niece of Richard Abernethie.
    I:32
Shannon, Christine ("Chrissie"). Diner at adjoining table to
    Barton party. VII:2
Shapland, Ann. Secretary to Miss Bulstrode. I:35
Sharpe, __ . Police inspector. I:33
Shaw, __ . Joint bank manager; alias: Ventnor. I:3:e
Shaw, Dr. __ . Physician at inquest. XI:9
Sheldon, Rose. Hotel chambermaid; former actress. II:11
Sheppard, Caroline. Older sister of Dr. S. I:4
Sheppard, Dr. James. Narrator; country physician. I:4
Shoreham, Robert. A top scientist. XI:10
Shrivenham, Lionel. British embassy employee in Baghdad. XI:7
Simmons, Miss __ . Housemaid at the Angkatells. I:25
Simmons, Archdeacon __ . Friend of Pennyfather. II:11
Simmons, Julia. "Distant cousin" of Miss Blacklock; real name:
    Emma Jocelyn Stamfordis. II:5
Simmons, Patrick. "Distant cousin" living with Miss Blacklock.
    II:5
__ , Simone. A medium. I:37:g
Simpson, __ . Bank employee; lodger with Mrs. Todd. I:30:i
Simpson, Alec. Naval lieutenant. I:30:b
Simpson, Alexander. Art gallery proprietor. I:26:j
Sims, __ . Police inspector. I:20:e
Sims, __ . House builder and decorator. II:14
Sims, Doris. Manikin at Ambrosine's. I:10
Skinner, Emily. Younger of the Skinner sisters. I:29:d
Skinner, Lavinia. Elder of the Skinner sisters. I:29:d
Slack, __ . Police inspector at Much Benham. I:29:c; II:1,3
Slattery, Mrs. __ . Housekeeper to Dr. Lord's predecessor. I:22
Slicker, __ . House agent in Market Basing. III:4
Small, Florence. A Girl Guide who knew Pamela Reeves. II:3
Smethurst, Capt. __ . Troubled officer in Damascus. IV:1:h
Smith, Ivor. Old friend of Tommy's in Intelligence. III:4
Snell, __ . Butler to Chevenix-Gore. I:17:c
Sobek. Second oldest son of Imhotep. XI:5
Soloman, __ . Proprietor of used-book store. I:39
Somers, Miss __ . Inefficient typist. II:7
Somervell, Maj. __ . Buyer of Mrs. Welman's house. I:22
__ , Sonia. Secretary to Sir Roderick Horsefield. I:41
Sopworth, Alice. Sister of Claud S. XI:3:k
Sopworth, Clara. Sister of Claud S. XI:3:k
Sopworth, Claud. Rival of James Bond. XI:3:k
Sopworth, Dorothy. Sister of Claud S. XI:3:k
Southwood, Hon. Joanna. Friend of Linnet Ridgeway; second

Stevens, ___ . Butler to Jimmy Thesiger. VI:2

Stevens, Charles. Detective inspector. I:26:m

Stillingfleet, Dr. John. Psychiatrist; friend of Poirot. I:36:e; I:41

Stirling, Pamela. Girl friend of David Ardingly. VIII:1

Stoddart, Dr. Michael. Young physician. I:26:i

Stoddart-West, Lady ___ . Mother of James S.-W.; see Martine. II:8

Stoddart-West, James. Young friend of Alexander Eastley. II:8

Stokes, Dr. ___ . Delicensed physician. II:11

Stokes, Dr. ___ . Police doctor at Jocelyn St. Mary. II:13

Stone, ___ . Chief constable at Hurst St. Cyprian. I:35

Stone, Dr. ___ . Archeologist. II:1

Stonor, Gabriel. Secretary to Renauld; English. I:2

Strange, ___ . Mining engineer. I:12

Strange, Mrs. Audrey. First wife of Nevile S. VI:4

Strange, Sir Bartholomew. Harley Street specialist in nervous disorders. I:10

Strange, Nevile. Rich, athletic young man. VI:4

Strange, Mrs. Nevile (Kay). Second wife of Nevile S. VI:4

Stranleigh, Lady Barbara ("Babs"). Often-married baroness. V:1:g

Stravinska, Anna. Ballet dancer; French. II:8.

Streptitch, Count Feodor Alexandrovitch. Possible employer of job applicants. XI:3:g

Strete, Mrs. Mildred. Daughter of Carrie Louise Serrocold; widow. II:6

Stroud, Charmian. Fiancee of Edward Rossiter. I:29:b

Stroud, Mary. Employee at Black Swan. I:12

Stubbs, Sir George. Rich businessman; owner of Nasse House. I:34

Stubbs, Lady Hattie. Wife of Sir George S. I:34

Stylptitch, Count ___ . Prime Minister of Herzoslovakia; statesman; deceased. VI:1

Subayska, Mme. ___ . Slav woman in Mrs. Jeffries' train compartment. IV:1:g

Sugden, ___ . Police superintendent. I:19

Suleiman, Abdul. Iraqi boatman. XI:7

Summerhaye, ___ . Police superintendent. I:1

Summerhayes, Maj. Johnnie. Husband of Mrs. Maureen S. I:31

Summerhayes, Mrs. Johnnie (Maureen). Guest house manager. I:31

Summerhayes, Mrs. Maureen. Mutual friend of Poirot and Mrs. Upjohn. I:35

___ , Susanne. Former nursery maid to Daisy Armstrong. I:9

Sutcliffe, Angela. Actress; dinner guest of Cartwright. I:10

Sutcliffe, Mrs. Henry (Joan). Sister of Bob Rawlinson. I:35

Sutcliffe, Jennifer. Daughter of Mrs. Joan S. I:35

Swartz, Gertrud. Old servant to Dr. Rosen; German. I:38:g

Sweetman, Mrs. ___ . Village postmistress. I:31

Tomlinson, Jean. Resident at hostel. I:33
Toredo, Angélica. Cabaret dancer in Ramat; Spanish. I:35
Tosswill, Dr. __ . British Museum official. I:3:f
Totman, __ . Newspaper dealer in Chipping Cleghorn. II:5
Trapp, Hiram P. Wealthy man in love with Jeanne Beroldy; American. I:2
Tredwell, __ . Waverly butler. I:29:g
Tredwell, __ . Butler at Chimneys. VI:1,2
Trefusis, Emily. Fiancée of James Pearson. X:1
Trefusis, Owen. Secretary to Sir Reuben Astwell. I:36:c
Trelawny, __ . Lady Tressilian's lawyer. VI:4
Trent, Mrs. Claire. Hostess at dinner party. I:28:b
Trent, Hugo. Nephew of Chevenix-Gore. I:17:c
Trent, Jack. Husband of Mrs. Claire T. I:28:b
Trenton, Charles. See "Enoch Arden." I:27
Tressilian, Lady Camilla. Widow of Sir Matthew T.; aristocratic invalid. VI:4
Tressilian, Edward. Elderly butler. I:19
Trevelyan, Capt. Joseph Arthur. Builder of Sittaford House. X:1
Treves, Dr. __ . Physician to Templeton. I:5
Treves, __ . Elderly barrister; specialist in criminology. VI:4
Tripp, Isabel. Sister of Julia T. I:15
Tripp, Julia. A medium. I:15
Trollope, Miss __ . Resident of same rooming house with the Sanders. II:2:j
Trotter, __ . Berkshire "detective sergeant." I:29:a
Tucker, Alfred. Farm laborer; father of Marlene T. I:34
Tucker, Mrs. Alfred. Mother of Marlene T. I:34
Tucker, Marlene. A Girl Guide who has central role in a Murder Hunt game. I:34
Tuckerton, Mrs. Thomas. Mother of Tommy T.; widow. VIII:1
Tuckerton, Thomasina Ann ("Tommy"). Girl who got in fight at Luigi's. VIII:1
Turner, Josephine. Second cousin and closest friend of Ruby Keene. II:3

Underhay, Capt. Robert. First husband of Mrs. Gordon Cloade. I:27
Unkerton, __ . Host at house party. V:1:b
Unkerton, Mrs. __ . Hostess at house party. V:1:b
(Unnamed). Fictitious sister of Desmond Lee-Wortley. I:36:a
(Unnamed). Resident of mountaintop villa; widow of English swimmer who drowned. V:1:k
(Unnamed). Man who followed Father Gorman. VIII:1
(Unnamed). Ferryman. IX:1
Upjohn, Mrs. __ . Mother of girl at school. I:35
Upjohn, Julia. New girl at school. I:35
Upward, Mrs. Laura. Former employer of Mrs. McGinty. I:31

Wade, Gerald ("Gerry"). Guest at Chimneys; Foreign Office employee. VI:2

Wade, Iris. An unhappy wife. IV:1:d

Wade, Loraine. Half-sister of Gerald W. VI:2

Wade, Reginald. Man whose wife wanted a divorce. IV:1:d

Wadell, Detective Sgt. __ . An investigator after the murder. II:11

Wagstaff, __ . Police inspector. I:26:1

Wainwright, Derek. Suitor of Sylvia Carslake. I:20:h

Waite, __ . Detective constable. II:7

Wake, Alfred. Vicar at Wychwood church. VI:3

Wales, Emma. Housemaid to Lady Tressilian. VI:4

Walker, Col. __ . Tour passenger; retired army officer. II:13

Wallace, Rube. Film actor. XI:3:j

Walters, Mrs. Esther. Secretary to Jason Rafiel; widow. II:10

Walton, __ . Chauffeur to Virginia Reed. VI:1

Wanstead, Prof. __ . Tour passenger; medical pathologist-psychologist. II:13

Warburton, Capt. Jim. Masterton's agent and errand boy. I:34

Wargrave, Alfred James. A rose grower. I:22

Wargrave, Justice Lawrence John. Judge of long experience. XI:4

Waring, Harold. Cabinet undersecretary. I:26:g

Warren, Dr. __ . Physician at Exhampton. X:1

Warren, Angela. Half-sister of Carla Crale. I:24

Waterhouse, Edith. Sister of James W. I:39

Waterhouse, James. Next-door neighbor of Miss Pebmarsh; worked in solicitor's office. I:39

Waverly, Johnnie. Kidnapped boy. I:29:g

Waverly, Marcus. Father of Johnnie W. I:29:g

Waverly, Mrs. Marcus (Ada). Mother of Johnnie W. I:29:g

Waynflete, Honoria. Elderly spinster. VI:3

Weardale, Adm. Sir Harry. First Sea Lord. I:30:h

Weardale, Lady Juliet. Wife of Adm. W. I:30:h

Weardale, Leonard. Son of Adm. W. I:30:h

Weatherby, Pauline. Sister-in-law of Barton Russell. I:20:e

Webb, Bella. Cook for Thyrza Grey. VIII:1

Webb, (Rosemary) Sheila. Typist at secretarial school. I:39

Weissgarten, Dr. __ . Hebrew scholar; cleric. II:11

Welch, Inspector __ . Police officer. I:36:f

Wells, __ . Lawyer. I:1

Wells, __ . Local police officer at Churston. I:12

Wells, Elizabeth. Inglethorp maid. I:1

Welman, Mrs. Laura. Aunt of Elinor Carlisle; widow. I:22

Welman, Roddy (Roderick). Fiancé of Elinor Carlisle. I:22

Welsh, Joe. Farmhand on Gardner farm in Cornwall. IV:1:f

Welsham, Duchess of. Friend of Miss Bulstrode. I:35

Welwyn, David. Old friend of the Laceys. I:36:a

West, Sir Alington. An alienist. I:28:b

Williamson, Ted. Village garage mechanic. I:26:d
Willoughby, Dr. __ . Physician interviewed by Poirot. I:43
Willows, Dick. Pal of Franz Ascher. I:12
Wilmott, Randolph. U.S. ambassador to Court of St. James's.
    III:2:p
Wilson, Alfred. Son of William W. I:7
Wilson, Gilmour. Renowned chess player; American. I:5
Wilson, John. Guest in Déroulard house. I:3:n
Wilson, William. Gardener at End House. I:7
Wilson, Mrs. William (Ellen). Maid-cook at End House. I:7
Wimborne, __ . Crackenthorpe solicitor. II:8
Winburn, __ . Father of Mrs. Lancaster. XI:1:e
Windlesham, Lord Charles. Possible fiancé of Linnet Ridgeway.
    I:16
Windyford, Dick. Former suitor of Alix King Martin. I:28:g
Winkfield, __ . Police inspector. I:38:i; V:1:b
Winterspoon, Henry. Authority on rare poisons. I:11
Withers, Jessie. Waverly nurse. I:29:g
Wizell, Fred. Former gardener for the Ravenscrofts. I:43
Woddell, Agnes. Maid at Symmingtons; friend of Partridge. II:4
Wood, J. Baker. Collector of miniatures; American. I:37:a
Woodworth, Gen. Lord __ . Father of Patricia Brice-Woodworth.
    VII:2
Woolman, Janet. Leonides parlormaid. XI:6
Worrit, Mrs. __ . Cook for Nye. XI:10
Wren, Christopher. Tenant at Monkswell Manor; presumed
    architect. I:29:a
Wright, Gerald. Schoolteacher; possible fiancé of Elaine Fortescue.
    II:7
Wu Ling. Chinese merchant in Burma. I:3:m
Wyatt, Capt. __ . Invalid renter of a Trevelyan cottage. X:1
Wycherley, Nina. Gushing vacationer on Majorca; English. I:20:d
Wye, Maud. Friend of Sylvia Keene. II:2:k
Wylde, Martin. Gentleman convicted of murder. V:1:d
Wynward, Prof. __ . British Museum cipher expert. VI:1

Yahmose. Oldest son of Imhotep. XI:5
Yardly, Lady Maude. Hostess to Mary Marvell. I:3:a
Yoaschbim, __ . New tenor singing at Covent Garden. I:38:h

Zara. A clairvoyant. I:30:g
Zarida. A psychic who warned Mrs. Pritchard of danger. I:38:f
__ , Zelie. See Mlle. Meaupourat. I:43
Zerkowski, Countess Renata. Girl who switched identities with
    Nye; aliases: Mary Ann, Daphne Theodofanous. XI:10
Zeropoulos, __ . Parisian antique dealer. I:11
Zielinsky, Ella. Secretary to Jason Rudd. II:9
Zobeida. Small-time dancer. I:37:h